PROJECT ONE

PROJECT ONE

FOUNDATION ONE: THE FEMININE RESONANCE

ALISON STORM

Waterside Productions

Printed in the United States of America

First Printing, 2020

ISBN-13: 978-1-949001-14-3 print edition
ISBN-13: 978-1-949001-15-0 ebook edition

Waterside Productions

2055 Oxford Ave
Cardiff, CA 92007
www.waterside.com

TABLE OF CONTENTS

INTRODUCTION
MY PERSONAL NARRATIVE

In the winter of 2012, while leading a financially rewarding life in the high-fashion world of New York City, I became aware of the emptiness of the life I was living on the "hamster wheel" that so many imagine is the key to fulfillment. On December 12, at the age of thirty-three, I crumbled under these demanding cultural standards; however, on that day, my failures also became my greatest gifts. I woke up to an inner explosion that tore through everything I thought I was: it was a full-blown kundalini awakening. This led me to witnessing what many refer to as Samadhi, or Heaven on Earth, in a mere twenty-four hours. I tell people that I was delirious, but I had to get to that state to "lose my mind" and find God. I entered into a reclusive life for eight months before later meeting my partner, and now-husband, Jonny Podell.

———

But it was now July 2019, and a lot had changed ... .

Jonny and I were on the cusp of separation. Our long-winded power struggle had reached its climax. Our house was being put up for sale, I was fleeing to my parents' home for comfort, and our toddler was reluctant to cooperate with ... *anything.*

I felt confused, distressed, and mostly sad. I wanted answers. Was this right? Was it all a mirage? Was my marriage false? Were we ever really soul mates? What was I going to do with my life?

Everything since my spontaneous and glorious awakening back in 2012 had seemed to vanish within a short six years. Here I was on this journey with a person I loved dearly, but who couldn't function within my life. My vision was clouded with confusion, and the clear perception that I'd once embodied had disappeared.

Darkness had blinded me, and now I was left feeling mystified. How had this even happened? Where had I gone wrong? Somehow ... I'd given away my Free Will.

What needed to happen? I'd received an important message that month—a divine message. It told me to unconditionally love in the face of adversity, rejection, criticism, and pain. Most important, I needed to love when it hurt the most; and when suffering, to love the perpetrator. I was being urged to swallow the pride, the pain, the hurt ... and to make the hard choice in the moment of that pain to choose love. And, above all, I needed to ask God to take my pain and transmute it into unconditional love.

I took that message and made it my reality, as did Jonny. Within twenty-four hours, I received a waterfall of love that washed over me and allowed me to feel the light of God coursing through my family and me. My vision became clear once again, and we unified as *ONE*. My confusion vanished. Jonny and I performed the seemingly impossible—an alchemical process whereby we transmuted all darkness into light.

From there, I entered into a higher dimensional space. My reality became that of God, and I aligned to my truth once again.

I began waking up at 3:33 A.M. every day. I knew something was happening, but I wasn't clear what it was.

Two months later, in October, Jonny and I were driving north to Montreal, where we'd planned to celebrate my fortieth birthday. As we traveled, we both received messages. Mine was that this year would mark the time when I would pass my personal lifelong test to love unconditionally. With this goal finally under my belt, I would now be prepared to fully realize my role as a channel (a person who serves as a medium). The year 2020 would also be the time when masses of people, such as Jonny and me, would come into unity as *ONE*.

During that trip to Montreal, Jonny had an experience where he felt God within everything he was witnessing and feeling. He knew he was at ONE with God and found great peace as a result.

Three weeks after my birthday, a new energy unexpectedly came through and introduced itself to me as *The Forces of Higher Collective Consciousness*. It asked me to begin dictation on what would be called *Project ONE*. It informed me that it would take me three months to dictate this project, and it would be available to the public in 2020.

And sure enough, three months later I completed the dictation and began the process of transcription. The book was fully transcribed on March 12, 2020, and it went on its way to my agent—one week prior to the coronavirus outbreak in the US. My book would be released to the public just in the nick of time for humanity.

Now you are reading this very book…and for good reason. You've been prepared to receive the information that I'm presenting here, and I assure you that you'll know what to do with it once you're done.

The energy I channel states repeatedly, "Free Will [I'm using initial caps throughout to emphasize the importance of this concept] is the gift of humanity. If you do not know where you have an opportunity to use your Free Will throughout your day, than you have given away your Free Will. Without using your Free Will, the higher energies cannot help you."

I know now that *Project ONE* would not be possible without that one crucial choice to love my husband in the face of any hurt feelings and pain, and to always put him first. And it took his commitment as well. It was that simple. With that one choice…God took over the rest.

This is why when people ask me, "So are *you* the channel for *Project ONE*?" I reply, "No, I am partnering with Jonny on this project." The reason is that, energetically, we both brought this project to fruition by accessing our Free Will. We opened an energetic gateway so that I could disseminate this work. It could not be done any other way.

So as you read this material, I ask you to take a long, hard look at your life, which is a prerequisite for being a part of *Project ONE*. See where you have an opportunity to access your Free Will. Determine where you have the most difficult time loving other human beings. Know that, most likely, they're living with you in your household, right under your nose. You may say that you love them, but how do you *treat* them?

Finally, please understand the *meaning* of unconditional love. You cannot say you love other people and then judge or diminish their behavior. You cannot claim love for others and then get angry because they didn't do something for you, or they did it in a way that was different from what you expected. You cannot love others and then choose to feel hurt by their (sometimes) unconscious words. Most important, it is not unconditional love when you feel sad or despondent as a result of others' actions. All you need to do is simply *love*. We only have each other. Without one another, we have nothing. So, I urge you to treat all of the individuals in your life as if they're your lifelines … because that's exactly what they are.

As I embarked upon the task of being the channel for *Project ONE*, a new type of healing began to unfold. Faulty programs within myself were brought into realignment, which was only able to occur through Free Will, my commitment to the information I was receiving and presenting … and, of course, God.

So now, my hope is that this work brings you the healing that you have sought, but above all else, I hope this work brings all of humanity the healing that we need.

This is the next phase of human evolution, and as we move forward as a species, we can only truly move forward as *ONE*.

With Love,
Ali

Editorial note: There are no rules as to how you read or absorb each part of this book, or each individual "record." You might want to read several records a day, or just work on one per day, slowly absorbing the concepts. And, you may find that upon rereading each record over a period of time, you will get more and more out of the material. Know that your intuition will tell you what's best for you.

And a grammatical mention: To avoid awkward "he/she" and "him/her" constructions, "their," "they" and "them" are often used to refer to singular antecedents.

PART ONE

THE FEMININE
RESONANCE

RECORD 1

THE MISSION

What you, the reader, can know is that you can resume *Project ONE* now. Why the word *resume*? Because you have already begun this project. Through the process of your recent life, you have begun the work of this project, and the energetic field you inhabit has changed. This project will not only benefit you, but it will benefit *all* of humanity. This will be an energetic transmission to benefit all of humanity.

Now, there will be words in this project, but in addition to the words, there will be an energetic coding, if you wish to call it that. This energetic coding of the planet is being altered now. As you realize that everything in your life has prepared you to change along with the energetic coding of the planet, you will understand how it has impacted your own personal reality.

Why is this significant? You have been discussing this for years as a society. Specifically, society has been discussing the healing of the masculine and feminine energy for years. But what does this mean to *your* society? What is coming forth for humanity is not only the healing of the masculine and the feminine energy—and these two energies coming together in unity—it is a lower energetic frequency that is being dissipated.

The only way the lower energetic frequency is being dissipated is by embodying in the higher energetic frequencies. These higher energetic frequencies are here now to bring forth the support needed for humanity. Humanity has its own Free Will, you see. Through its own Free Will, it has to make the choice for this to be so, but it cannot be done if the choice is not made by the human species.

The human species has to make the choice of love. As the human species makes this choice, as it shakes its head yes, as it says yes to this choice, the higher energies can then come in and support the human species in this great change.

So, what has to happen now? What has to happen now is not just teaching, because teaching alone will not work for the human species. There have been many teachings for thousands of years showing how humans can come into their own unity with God, into their own unity with self. But what has to happen now is an energetic reprogramming in your system. This energetic code that is changing now is being changed through many vessels and projects, such as *Project ONE*.

There will be many projects being brought forth now. You ask, "Okay, what is *Project ONE*?" Well, the project that will be brought forth will unfold in the activation of many right now who will be bringing forth their higher intuitive abilities.

If you wish to begin now, we can. *Project ONE. Project ONE.* This is what it will be called: *Project ONE.*

RECORD 2

THE FEMININE RESONANCE

There are two terms to discuss today. There is woman, and there is the feminine. There is also the feminine working through women. That is what we are speaking of, the feminine energy working through women.

When we say the word *feminine*, we are speaking of the feminine energy. When we say the word *woman*, we are speaking of the female human species.

What is the feminine energy here to do today? First, we describe the feminine energy by explaining to you that the feminine energy does work through women *and* men.

The feminine energy consists of energetic resonances within the human female. These energetic resonances occur differently in the male. So, while there is an energetic frequency, a feminine frequency within the male and female, the resonance of the feminine energy within the female is different from the energetic resonance of the feminine energy within the male. People believe that the feminine energy is the same within the male and female. It is *not* the same within the male and female. There is a different energetic resonance within the female and within the male.

There are fine differences between the two resonances. These energetic resonances that are carried through the human body are simultaneously different and alike.

Today, we are discussing the feminine resonance within the female body. We say the female body because that is what carries the resonance. The female body is the vehicle for the resonance to be carried on this physical plane. The feminine resonance does not exist if the female body is not here to carry that feminine resonance.

There is an awakening to what the female body truly is, and that is a temple of God. People are beginning to understand this. What they do not understand is that the feminine resonance within the female body has been distorted for some time.

Now, as the feminine resonance has been distorted, you may ask yourself, "Okay, well, how does the feminine resonance become healed again?" First, you must understand what the feminine resonance is.

This energetic frequency within the female body consists of love, nurturing, compassion, and receiving. Yes, it does consist of all these energies that you traditionally know the Divine Feminine to consist of. But what you do not understand is the acute understanding of what this feminine resonance is.

The feminine resonance is not something that can be described in words. It is only something that can be described in energy. It is felt in the essence of the female. It is felt when *you* are the female. The female right now has lost touch with what the feminine resonance truly is, although it lives inside her.

This feminine resonance, if you wish to call it that, is something divinely beautiful. It is something of God. It is the female form of God. This has been known throughout time, and many religions have attempted to depict what this feminine resonance truly is. And again, this is beyond what the mind can comprehend, meaning you cannot use your mind to access this knowledge.

You feel the feminine resonance with a mother who has just given birth. When you go into a room with a mother who has just given birth and she has a child in her arms, you can hug her, and you can feel the feminine resonance. This is the resonance of a Divine Mother. Yes, it is. It is the energetic frequency of a woman who has given birth and has a child in her arms, and she says, "Yes, I will love and care for this child in the face of all adversity and pain. This is my one priority." The Divine Mother, however, loves every human being on the planet as she loves a child that she has just given birth to, and she has the capacity to endure any type of pain or adversity for all those around her, with great love.

That feminine resonance is fierce. It is divine. It is courageous. It is brave. It is willing to say no to everybody else in the face of struggle for the child. This feminine resonance that exists within all women does not exist within the male body. It only exists within the female body.

The only way to access the feminine resonance is through an activation. Now, this energetic activation is not only an activation because the feminine resonance has been within the female body since the inception of the female body; it is also a healing.

The feminine resonance will know itself as healed once the female body is healed. The female body is actually the mirror of the female form of feminine resonance. That is what the female body is: a mirror of the feminine resonance.

The feminine resonance will be the groundwork for how this project will evolve.

As of now, the female body has been processing healing over time; however, there is an urge, there is a need, for this to happen more quickly. As this happens at an accelerated pace, the feminine resonance can move into its rightful seat.

So, how do you do this? They work in symbiosis, the feminine resonance and the female body. This can be done through the conscious mind saying, "Yes, I wish this to be done." But that is all the conscious mind can really do in this process.

How does the female say yes to the feminine resonance within her? The female says yes to the feminine resonance within her by saying no to the distortion that she has agreed to for thousands of years. How does she say no to the distortion that she has agreed to for thousands of years? She begins to understand the lie within herself.

She begins to understand that there has been a lie within herself, and she sees the lie outpictured on her body. Her body is the form that says yes or no. This is how she knows if the feminine resonance is healed within—it is through her body saying yes or no. Her body will tell her if she has agreed to the lie or not.

How will her body tell her? Her body will tell her through how she has agreed to the demands of society, to what society has told her. If she has felt the pressure of society and the denial of society, and if she has felt the suppression of society and the pain or rage of society, it will be shown in her body.

She knows now that her body will tell her yes or no. If her body tells her no, she can say, "Okay, well, I am not going to agree anymore to what I've been told." This is what she will do. She will begin to speak for herself. She will begin to speak for the feminine resonance within her. As she begins to hear this voice within her, she can begin to say yes to the feminine resonance.

This resonance, while it is been distorted, has the ability to be healed immediately, as it is already whole in the higher dimensions. This does not need to take a long time. However, what it does take is for the willingness of the female to be able to say no to the distortion that she has agreed to for thousands of years. This is her Free Will at hand.

Now, this may not be an easy thing to do. It takes tremendous courage and power for the female to say no. But what can happen is that as the females begin to say no to the distortion that has been agreed to for thousands of years, they come together and support each other in this process. As they come together to support each other in this process, it becomes easier. This is the precursor to Collective Evolution, which will be discussed in more detail later in this book.

As the females say no to the distortion that they've agreed to for thousands of years, they can say, "Okay, well, what is this feminine resonance within me that needs to be healed?" As you begin to say no to the lower energies, it's much easier for the higher energy to come in.

The feminine resonance is carried in the male body as well. However, as mentioned before, this feminine resonance is different in the female body than it is in the male body. So again, as we say that the feminine energy is within all male and female bodies, the feminine resonance within the female body is quite different from the feminine resonance within the male body.

When you come into the essence of who the Divine Mother is, the feminine resonance is pure. This is the potential of the feminine resonance within the female. The strength of the Divine Mother is a miracle, and this is the miracle that lives inside all women. The Divine Mother is the essence of the *woman*.

RECORD 3

CODE 333

What will be discussing today? So far we have touched on the feminine resonance and what this means to the female body, the female population, and what this means to humanity as a whole. Now we will go further into what the feminine resonance is, and what this means for the time you are embarking upon.

Why does the feminine resonance seek to be expressed today? The time we are embarking on is more of a process that humanity is going through, to be able to emerge on the other side in a new light.

The feminine resonance is the component that will help humanity throughout this period. Now, how it helps humanity through this period is because it is expressive and capable of dissipating other energies.

At this time, we will discuss energetic codes. Each cell that is within the human body is a microcosm of the macrocosm that is the universe. The physical cell consists of energy. This energy that the cell is made of is coded. Therefore, the energy that the cell is made of is preprogrammed.

There are two components to altering energy. This is the human Free Will along with God. Now, when we speak of God, we are talking about the Resonance of All Creation. That is what we mean when we speak of God. Humanity cannot understand God through the mind; therefore, we simply explain God as the Resonance of All Creation.

The cells vary within each human being, but they are also alike—similar to how the feminine resonance is different within the female body and the male body. Each human being is unique in their DNA makeup and their resonance system. However, they are also the same. What you do all hold in common is that divine makeup. Now, this divine makeup within you does have an energetic code. This energetic code is the same within every single human being, the code of one. This is why you often say, "We are all the same. We are not different." You all have this common DNA makeup, which is the physical reflection of the resonance system.

You also have different energy systems within each of you, so while you are all the same, you are also all unique. To be able to alter energy within the universe, you have to understand what the code is.

What is the code of the feminine resonance? Each resonance carries its own code. Numbers are within the code. But there is more to the code than numbers alone. The code of the feminine resonance is 333.

As you understand coding and science, you will understand the soul. However, you will not be able to understand science with your mind alone. You will only be able to further advance your science with the work of the soul. You can only go so far with the mind. The soul will come in to teach you.

This is only the beginning for you. Your science right now is held in limitation because you are held in limitation from not being able to access your own cellular structure. This is the imprisonment that you have all struggled with. You are learning how to unlock codes so that you can begin to liberate yourselves into freedom—freedom as a divine soul.

The Divine Mother feminine resonance code is 333. This has been powerfully symbolic to you and many others throughout time. That is because this is the code of the feminine resonance. The codes will work with you if you learn how to work with the codes as well. It can be done in symbiosis. You can work with the codes, and the codes can work with you.

If you can begin to understand these codes, the code of 333 is the code of the feminine resonance. So, how do you begin to work with this code? First, you begin to acknowledge that the code exists within you. This concept of a code may seem ambiguous.

Bring awareness to the code within itself. Understand that there is an operating system working within you. You are the operating system. That is what you are as the human vessel. You have been held in limitation now for thousands of years, and now it is time for you to liberate yourself, or unlock the door to be able to express yourself as the full self that you are.

This resonance within you of *ONE* has been held in secrecy for so long that it has not been able to be expressed because there has been an operating system within you that has not allowed this to be so. The energetic codes of the universe have also been locked for a very long time, and they are now being changed.

Again, there are two components to unlock these codes. That is God and your Free Will. Now, the component of God has always been here. However, it is your Free Will that has not enabled you to access it within you.

So, you ask, "What is causing us from not making the choice?" It is the preprogrammed data within you.

So, right now, what this project will be doing is showing you how to unlock these codes through your Free Will. Now, you say, "We make this choice every day. We've been trying, and it feels like a struggle."

How do you begin to unlock the code through the Free Will? That is what we will be discussing. And as we discuss this, we will return back to the feminine resonance, the resonance of 333. But first, you must begin to understand how to unlock the code within you. Yes, you must have awareness that you are preprogrammed, that you are an operating system.

You say, "Okay, but we've had this component of love. We've had this component of God. We bring love into our lives every single day." But yet at the same time, you do not. You do not. It is your Free Will to choose love. Yes, it is. God and love have been here waiting for you. However, you do not choose it.

Now, yes, these programs within the energetic structure of your cells can be shifted through energy work. There are many people on the planet today who are doing energy work, who are attempting to transform the cellular data within you through love. Yes, this is happening. However, if the person's Free Will is not released to be able to say yes to the process, then it will not work. You will continue to go back to the programs within you, the preprogrammed data within yourselves, because it is who you believe you are.

The resonance of one, this cellular data within you, has been locked. You have known it to be dormant. Therefore, you keep reverting back to the other programs within you because those programs are dominating. You ask, "How is that possible? If God is the highest frequency, then how are the other programs dominating? How is this possible?"

The programs that have been operating within you for far too long have built into a mass. If you could understand a tumor within a body, you would understand that this mass has built up within the collective society. So, how do you begin to remove this mass? Again, through Free Will. This is the only way.

Once the human species decides that this is a choice, they will begin to decide something new. Through Free Will, yes, you say you choose it, but you really have not. This is where you are becoming blinded as you continue to go back to what you have been programmed to believe. This is a program that runs inside your mind. It is a program that runs inside your thoughts. It is what you believe you are. You have to begin to deprogram yourself. How do you allow that to happen?

RECORD 4

THE WOMB

What are we going to discuss today? Well, there are going to be many parts to *Project ONE*. First, we are laying the foundation for what will be a multilayered teaching and project. This project will be multidimensional.

What is the intention of *Project ONE*? The intention of *Project ONE* is to bring the feminine resonance into its wholeness and be restored on the planet again. That is the intention of *Project ONE*. There will also be many other components, but right now let us just be concerned with *Project ONE*, the feminine resonance.

As we have discussed, there are energetic codes that represent the cellular data that exists within you. What we are just beginning to explain is that the energetic codes represent cellular data, and you have the ability to change this data. Again, you are the operating system. The cellular data within you is what makes the operating system run. These programs within you are what make the operating system run. This is what makes life run. And now, you are at a place where you are changing these energetic codes.

So, what will you be doing? We are going to return back to the code of the feminine resonance, represented by the code of 333. What does this mean?

This energy that is making up the mother, the mother of the feminine resonance, the Divine Mother, this is Divine Mother energy. You have seen and encountered and understand that there is a Divine Mother. You have known what the Divine Mother may be. There have been women who have walked this plane who have embodied the essence of the Divine Mother. Now, how was it that they were able to do so?

Every woman on this planet has the potential to be the Divine Mother. This is the resonance that lives within her, and her potential. Now, this does not mean that you do not show praise for the Divine Mother who has walked the planet before. This has nothing to do with that. This has nothing to do with religion or worship. What this has to do with is what every woman has the potential to be in this plane.

Now, this code of 333, this is the code to unlock the feminine resonance. So, what do you begin to do to be able to unlock the feminine resonance within you? What does the code 333 mean?

When many read these teachings, there will be confusion, because the number three has been symbolic for many ideas and energies over a period of time. Many of you have begun to understand the symbolism of three and what that means to the soul. However, the number three is used in a myriad of variations and formations.

So, while the code three, while the number three, can represent much of the soul, man, and God walking on this plane—the Christ Consciousness—the code 333 is very specific to the feminine resonance and the Divine Mother. Today we are not speaking of the Holy Trinity. We are speaking of 333. This is the number. This is the code of the feminine resonance. We will go on to explain more codes and what their resonances are for those codes in later projects, but for right now, we are just discussing the code of the feminine resonance.

If you look within the female body, you will begin to understand how the female body is a mirror of the feminine resonance. The female body is able to give birth, to bring life into this plane from the higher heavens. This is because the female body was created to be able to support this resonance. There is a difference between the female body and the male body, which reflects why the Divine Mother, why the feminine resonance, is the code of 333, the three-pointed triangle. You must look within the womb, where the feminine resonance lives. This is the heart center of the feminine resonance—and the sacred triangle.

Within the cells of the womb where the feminine resonance lives, there is a slight distortion. How did this happen? This happened through, again, ancestors' family lineages. It has been passed down for thousands of years into every human. Therefore, every child who is brought into this plane, every child who is incarnated into this life, passes through this womb; every child who passes into this life or lives in this womb is created within this womb space. The cells that the child is created with are the cells of the womb. Therefore, there is a distortion in every child who comes into this world. This is how the human species has existed.

The distortion is so acute that it is barely detectable, but yet at the same time, this distortion that is so small has caused significant imprisonment of the human species. Humanity is now at a juncture where it is a requirement for the woman's cellular data within her womb to be made whole.

RECORD 5

FREE WILL

Now, let us return to *Project ONE*.

The codes that we are discussing in *Project ONE* and how you as a human species will be able to access your cellular data going forward as a civilization is information that is new to the planet, so we will be laying the groundwork as to how to access the cellular data within you to be able to reprogram yourself.

There are many women who are accessing their higher selves. Their higher selves do contain information that can show them how to do this; however, it has become impossible to fully access the higher self with this preprogrammed energy within the cells. There are many energy workers on the planet right now, as we said before, who are transmitting energy that is shifting the cellular data within your cells. You experience this as energetic sensations moving through you that are rewiring your own cells. You know this to be true, but what you do not understand is that you have the ability to do this yourself without another person. This manual is giving you access to be able to change the cellular data yourself without having to rely on another to do it for you.

So, where do you go now with the feminine resonance? We left off discussing the womb and how it holds the heart of the feminine resonance. You are limited in your knowledge of the energetic centers within the body.

There are infinite energetic centers within the human body. Therefore, the energetic center is not limited to those small numbers of energetic centers that you know yourself to contain. As a matter of fact, each cell contains energetic centers within the individual cell itself. Imagine this. Imagine that each cell contains an infinite amount of energetic centers within the cell itself.

So now we go back to the womb space. We understand now that the womb space contains the heart chakra of the feminine resonance—the heart of the Divine Mother and who she is and what she is in her power, in her glory, and everything that she is to the human species. She is so vast, and again, she has been depicted by religions in the past. The feminine God has been depicted, and she lives within the womb of every female body.

Now, how do you begin to access the female God within the womb space? How do you access the data within the cells of the womb? You go into the womb space—not with your mind, but with intelligence of the soul. So you are not going to the womb space with the mind. You are not going to the womb space just within a meditation. You are going to the womb space with the intelligence of the soul.

How do you go into the womb space with the intelligence of the soul? You go into the womb space with the intelligence of the soul by *calling* on the intelligence of the soul. Now you ask, "Okay, what is the soul intelligence?" This is an imprint that lives within the soul. It is a multidimensional imprint that lives within the soul. It is eternal, the soul intelligence.

So you say, "I don't understand this. This sounds impossible. How can the soul be intelligent? I thought the mind was intelligent and the soul was at the heart." The soul is intelligent as well. The soul is the heart, and the heart carries intelligence within itself. The soul is a composite. The intelligence is a composite that is built upon the soul. After thousands of years of incarnating into lifetimes, the soul builds intelligence. You cannot go into it with the mind. It is an impossibility. Physics does not allow it. The reason is that the cellular data is of the energetic body.

Therefore, the only way you can access the cellular data is through your soul intelligence. So you say, "Well, this is impossible. If we can't access our knowing, if we can't access our wisdom, then how are we going to access the cellular data?" This is the first step. You are beginning to access this knowing within you right now. However, this is intelligence you have not trusted for so long.

As you call upon the intelligence of the soul, it will meet you. It will override the programs that are running through you right now, but you must use your Free Will to be able to access that soul intelligence. As you have not trusted it and you have not had faith in it, you have believed every lie that you have been told.

The programs have been allowed to run free within you. You have been running on this operating system for thousands of years. Now it is time to begin to access the soul intelligence again that has been waiting for you. As you access the soul intelligence, you will be able to work with it and use it to access the data within your cells.

Again, this is simple physics. You can only access soul intelligence through your Free Will. That is why we said before that there are two components to changing your cellular data. That is God ... and Free Will.

RECORD 6

WORKING WITH TIME

We will return to *Project ONE*, the feminine resonance, and calling upon the intelligence of the soul to be able to unlock those codes of the cellular data. Now, the soul intelligence is working *with* you and is *of* you. There are many components to the human body and the human consciousness. You have Free Will. God has given you Free Will to be able to use it. So you have the soul intelligence, and you also have Free Will.

Now, the soul intelligence is of God. This is eternity. The soul lives eternally, so anything of the soul is eternal. However, this Free Will that you have been given, this is part of humanity. The soul intelligence is eternal, and Free Will is of the human experience. It is not eternal. Therefore, because you have Free Will, you can always choose something different. When you understand that Free Will is choice, Free Will is the human choice, you must understand that you always have the ability to choose differently. There are many components to the human consciousness, but Free Will and soul intelligence can work together to access these codes. When you are able to access and unlock these codes, you can access the cellular data within the cells.

Free Will is of this life, and soul intelligence is eternal. So how do you work with both of these together?

Free Will is your gift, and it has been denied for a long time. It is something that you are now beginning to recognize as a choice that you can begin to claim into your power again. You begin by taking account-ability for every thought, every action, and every event in your life. These teachings are true, and have been given to you for thousands of years. Free Will can only be claimed once you take responsibility and accountability for who you are and what you are. Free Will is a choice that can be claimed into your own power. As you begin to make the choice to use your Free Will, understand that you yourself have the accountability to be able to claim love, to choose love as yourself, as who you are. This is who you are. You are of God.

You cannot call upon the soul intelligence without using your Free Will. Again, this is physics. Soul intelligence always lives with you for eternity when you come into this lifetime; it is an agreement that you can only access the soul intelligence with your Free Will. Many of you have denied this choice for thousands of years. It is simple. You access the soul intelligence with your Free Will.

Once you have chosen your soul intelligence, you go in to unlock the code to your cellular data. This is a lesson being laid out.

Returning to the feminine resonance and the code of 333 ... why is this so important? How are we going to begin to access this resonance within us? We have described now what the feminine resonance is. We have now described what the soul intelligence is. We have now described why it is important to be able to use your Free Will when accessing the soul intelligence to gain entryway to your actual cellular data, which contains the data that comprises the feminine resonance.

If we go back to the soul intelligence and the Free Will, the human Free Will and the soul intelligence, and we begin to work with both of these components to access the cells, what we can understand is that the cellular data of the feminine resonance is the time, 3:33. We can begin to work with time and space to be able to access the cells.

The code 333 exists within all of time and space. So if you look at 333, this is the code of the feminine resonance. So how do you begin to work with time and space to be able to access this information? When you sit upon 3:33 with the soul intelligence, you give your Free Will over to the soul intelligence, which is the highest part of the soul that lives within you. When you hand over the keys to the soul intelligence with 3:33, you can begin to access the feminine resonance. Your soul intelligence will guide you.

PART TWO

TERMINOLOGY AND CONCEPTS

RECORD 7
BLACK MATTER

The subject that we will be discussing today is space. Space in the universe.

You may ask, "Okay, why are we discussing space, and what does this have to do with the feminine resonance project?" Again, we will be taking this step by step, layer by layer. This is a multilayered project. There are going to be many intricate components to this project. We will return to each component many times throughout its course.

When we refer to space, we are referring to something very specific, and that is black matter. What does black matter consist of? There are currently dark holes in the universe that scientists have an awareness of. They understand these dark holes, to an extent. Now, why is it important to discuss these dark holes, and what are they? Black matter is a very important component to understand. The only way to begin to understand it is with soul intelligence. Soul intelligence is the link that will bring you the pieces you need to understand black matter, because black matter exists in the eternal universe, just as the soul does.

If you look at your physical body, the physical earth, and the physical universe, you understand that the universe reflects back to you what is inside you. You understand that the cosmos lives inside you; that the cosmic makeup, patterns, and systems all live inside you. This is something that scientists understand.

Therefore, black matter also lives inside you. However, black matter is not fully detectable within the three-dimensional scope. We are not able to understand it in the three-dimensional universe because it exists in the multidimensional universe. It exists in the higher dimensions, so you can only see this with the higher dimensional eyes or the higher dimensional mind, which is soul intelligence. You can only see black matter through soul intelligence.

You may be saying, "I feel like I'm going off in tangents from the feminine resonance." We will circle back to the feminine resonance when it is time. Right now, we must explain each topic and each component as far as what will be the full formula for later so that you can understand how to access and decode and reprogram cellular data. But you must first understand each component that will be a part of the formula to be able to do this.

So now we have determined that black matter exists multidimensionally. It does not exist in the three-dimensional eye. It cannot be perceived by the three-dimensional mind. So, there is little known and understood about black matter. All you know is that it exists. This is similar to the soul. All you know is that it exists, but you have not scientifically proven this.

You now understand that black matter lives inside you, and each human being carries black matter. Now, what consists within black matter is something that can be scientifically proven. As you begin to scientifically prove and understand the consistency of what black matter is, you will be able to scientifically prove and understand the consistency of soul intelligence as well.

Whatever you see outpictured, lives within you. This is a theory that you know as a civilization. This theory also applies in the multidimensional universe. You exist as a multidimensional being. Multidimensionally, whatever exists within you exists within the universe as well. This is what black matter is.

There are people now speculating about this who have begun to understand the phenomenon of black matter. However, it has not been proven in science, and that is what needs to happen to move forward as a society. Black matter needs to be understood from the multidimensional perspective before it can be studied, understood, and worked with.

Now, why is space and black matter important to understand for the formula, the feminine resonance project? This will be pertinent to the importance of soul intelligence.

Soul intelligence is a key component of this formula. Otherwise, the project cannot be done. The project that is being laid out cannot be done without soul intelligence. In order to understand soul intelligence, we are asking you to understand black matter and its consistency.

Now, how do you begin to access that higher dimensional mind so you can understand black matter? You cannot understand black matter if you do not understand soul intelligence. And you cannot understand soul intelligence if you do not understand black matter. So, where do you even begin? This is a question that humanity has studied for thousands of years: Where do you begin?

If you look at black matter, on a three-dimensional scope, on a physical scope, you understand that there is black matter. You now know you can only understand further with soul intelligence. So how, then, can you access that multidimensional human being? There are many humans on the planet who are working multidimensionally at this time.

You say, "Okay, this is confusing because the multidimensional universe consists of the physical universe. So how is it that black matter is the multidimensional universe when the multidimensional universe should include the physical universe?"

Understand that black matter is the physical component of the multidimensional universe. Black matter is physical, but it has a multidimensional purpose. Black matter does not have a physical purpose, but you understand it as a physical experience because black matter is in the physical dimension.

So, what is the multidimensional purpose of black matter? The purpose of black matter in the multidimensional universe is to simply hold a neutral space. It holds a neutral space. It is not light or dark. It is a neutrality, and this neutrality exists within you as well.

How does it exist within you, and why is it important to the formula that is going to be created to prove resonance? Neutrality exists within you in the multidimensional universe. It is not light, and it is not dark. It is a balancing space. Now, this neutrality that exists within you ... why is it important, and how does it work?

Within the physical body, black matter exists as energy and space. How does it exist as space within the physical body, and how does it exist within space within the multidimensional human being? Black matter exists in the physical universe, and it holds neutrality in the multidimensional universe. If you look to the physical human being, what black matter is, is nothing more than an energetic space that you hold.

If you look to the multidimensional human being, it is a neutrality. So, it is important to understand this, because as the formula for the feminine resonance is laid out, it is important to understand that you have the multidimensional human in neutral space. This neutral space is not feminine. It is not masculine. It is not light, and it is not dark. It is black matter. This neutral space works within you to balance you as a human. You would not be able to exist without this neutral space and energy.

Light energy needs dark energy to exist, and vice versa. When these two energies come together, there is a neutral space that is created. This neutral space acts as a barometer that exists within your energetic system. This is the black matter of the multidimensional human being. As this formula is laid out as the groundwork, you have to understand what this black matter will mean to the total formula.

As we begin to show you how to code or how to decode your cellular data, what you have to understand is what this black matter is to the code. If you look at the code of the cellular data, you can understand that each resonance is represented by a code. Each chord is represented by a number. The chords make up the resonance. The resonance consists of chords, and the chords are represented by numbers. The resonance is represented by numbers and shapes.

Now, what is the black matter doing to be able to support the resonance? What the black matter is doing to be able to support the resonance is to hold a neutral space for the resonance to exist. If there was no neutral space for the resonance to exist, the resonance would not be able to actually survive. The resonance would actually not be able to live. This is how it works. The resonance needs the neutrality to be able to live. The resonance actually needs that neutral space within the multidimensional human being to be able to live.

This neutral space within you is going to be a key component of the formula for the feminine resonance. And the resonance needs the neutrality to be able to live. Now, why you need to understand this is because you have to understand how the resonance works within your cells. The resonance works within your cells. Remember that the cells contain the entire universe. The cells actually contain the entire universe within each cell. So you can understand that this neutral space, this black matter, lives within each cell.

There are components to the cell that you do not understand scientifically, and those components to the cell are the black matter. This is nothing but neutral space consisting of energetic particles not detected by the physical mind. So as you begin to study this more, as we begin to lay out the formula for the feminine resonance, all you need to understand right now is that the neutral space or the neutrality is needed for the feminine resonance, or for any resonance, to exist.

RECORD 8

CODES

What we are going to discuss today is numerology. Why numerology? To you, the channel, numerology is something that you are not familiar with, and it is a practice that you do not consider legitimate. There is truth in numerology. Not all truth has been proven that is within numerology, but you have to understand that for the sake of this project, there is truth, there is validity, in some numerology.

Numerology has not been scientifically proven, and as a study it has not been made valid for the general public of human society. However, there is actual science behind numerology. And now, where humanity is going as a society, we will be able to prove the validity of certain topics, certain components that are within numerology.

To the channel, this is quite confusing because the channel does not know anything about numerology; however, you do not need to know about numerology to understand the importance of it to this project.

Geometry is one of those components. Geometry itself is within the mathematical studies of humanity. Now, geometry is also going to be very important to the outcome of this project. When you, the channel, become nervous, it is because these subjects, geometry and numerology, are very foreign to you.

How is it possible that geometry and numerology could be related? If you ask numerologists, they would understand this very well. However, since the channel is not a numerologist, which is okay because most people are not numerologists, this is an introductory topic. If you look at geometry, if you look at the shapes of many objects, they contain numerology within the shapes. This is how codes begin to work—through shapes and numbers—which is a key link to your cellular data.

You need to have a foundation of numerology and geometry to begin to understand the codes of cellular data. Now you are saying, "Wow! This is far beyond me. I don't even know how this is possible." We are going to take it one step at a time for you so that you will be able to understand. This is a layered teaching.

For the sake of this project, you do not need to understand what each number represents. This information has been widely misinterpreted throughout time by humanity. The fact that you do not know what each number represents is a positive. It is a good way to begin this project because you are beginning with a blank canvas.

Each number is something humanity knows and understands; and mind you, you know that numbers are infinite, and that within each number, there are infinite numbers. However, the numbers each represent a chord A of an energy, or better said, a resonance.

There are infinite combinations to these numbers and to the chords, and all of these chords and numbers represent various resonances. The chords make up the resonances. The numbers represent the resonances. That is why you have coded resonances. The numbers represent the chords, which make up the resonances. This is actually how the universe works. Now, humanity understands numbers; therefore, it will be easy to understand chords.

If you could understand that a chord is a component of a note of a song, it is a tone within the note. Now, you ask, "How does geometry come into this? If the numbers represent the chords that are within each resonance, then how is geometry a factor?"

If you look at a shape, any shape—a triangle, a circle, or a square— imagine the shape in your mind's eye. These shapes are all represented by numerical values through the measure of points and angles. You know this. This is simple math. This is very simple math that you learned when you were young.

So if the shape represents a number, and the number represents a chord, and the chord is within each resonance, and a resonance makes up millions of chords, then what is the shape to the resonance? That is what you have to ask yourself. The shape represents part of the code to the resonance. The number and the shape combined represent the code to the resonance. This is what you have to understand. If the resonance is made up by energetic chords, then the number and shape is the symbol for the resonance. It is the code for the resonance. That is what this is.

Now you ask, "How does each chord get assigned a number?" Well, this is universal. This is creation. Humanity was given numbers. Humanity was given the system of numbers to be able to understand creation. You have gone tremendously far in using numbers and math to understand the universe.

RECORD 9

MOTION

What will we be discussing today? Rotation. Why is rotation important to understand? What is rotation to the feminine resonance? And more important, what is rotation to the soul?

Rotation of the universe, rotation of the planet, and how much of matter moves in a rotational spin—we will show why that is important to the soul.

If you understand that particles or the substance of space move in rotation, that everything including space and matter is always moving in motion, then you are always moving in motion in a rotational pattern as well. And the cells that live within you are always in motion and often in rotation as well. There is a circular rotation that is happening within you, where you are always in movement. Energy is always in motion. This is a constant variable.

Again, if you look at the universe, you will see that the universe is free floating; however, much of it moves in rotational patterns—the sun, the moon, the earth, the sky. You will see that everything always moves in this rotational pattern. *You* are also moving in this rotational pattern.

As you are moving in this rotational pattern, the energy that you consist of is moving in a rotational pattern in the physical universe. You are moving in this rotational pattern in the multidimensional universe as well.

Remember, everything that exists in the physical universe also exists within the multidimensional universe. However, the physical universe is more dense than the multidimensional universe because of the particles moving at a slower rate of speed. This is due to no gravitational pull in the multidimensional universe. That is the difference. There is no gravitational pull, whereas there is a gravitational pull in the physical universe.

In the physical universe, your cells are in motion; it is important to understand this resonance theory. Now, this resonance theory says that there is an energetic system that is within you that lives within each cell in the multidimensional universe. Now, what you can understand is that if within each cell there is a rotational pattern occurring in the cells in the physical universe or in the physical body, then there is a pattern happening in the multidimensional universe as well. If there is something existing in the physical universe, then it is also existing in the multidimensional universe as well. So if you yourself exist in the physical universe, then you also exist in the multidimensional universe. If a cell exists in the physical universe, then this cell also exists in the multidimensional universe. If what is inside the cell exists in the physical universe, then what is inside the cell also exists in the multidimensional universe.

This is where the resonance or vibration lives. The resonance lives in the multidimensional universe within the cell. So what you can understand is that if the cell is moving in a rotational pattern, then the resonance is also moving in a rotational pattern. This is energy. This is how energy works. Energy is always in motion and in vibration. Whether it is in this universe or the multidimensional universe, it is always in motion.

This is important, as the movement of the cell and resonance is important to how the resonance sustains itself. The resonance is sustained by moving in constant. Now, what you may be asking is, "Why is the resonance sustained by moving in this rotational pattern, and why is the cell sustained by moving in this rotational pattern?" The universe is sustained by living in motion. You know this very well. Humanity has done a great job of looking outward, but again, right now we are using science to be able to look inward. You have used science to be able to look inward in the physical dimension, but you have not used science to look inward on the multidimensional universe within the multidimensional human.

There is a gap between science and spirituality, and the key link is being able to use science to look at the multidimensional human. The reason this gap exists is because you need to be able to use soul intelligence to access the multidimensional human. You cannot use soul intelligence without Free Will. We explained this earlier on in the project, and we will return to this as the project continues to unfold and develop. But for today, we just need to discuss what this rotational pattern is and why it is important to the resonance.

Motion and rotational patterns create life. Rotation is the pattern of the circle, and this is also the pattern of the soul. This is why the circle represents the soul. It is because the soul and the circle both have no end. This pattern is important to life, if you can understand that life has no end.

Now, what you can also understand is that this rotational pattern within resonance theory will be important because the resonance itself is an essence and in vibration. It is only something that can be felt. However, there is energy within this essence that exists in the multidimensional universe and is in motion.

This pattern that is occurring within the cell is the pattern of the resonance. So the vibration of the cell meets the vibration of the resonance. The resonance is an energy. Every resonance within every cell is in motion in a pattern, and there are many variations of resonances that make up these patterns. There are many various resonances that exist within the multidimensional human that form patterns. Now, why is this important, you ask? What you have to begin to understand is how the resonance works within you. And as you begin to understand how the resonance works within you, you can begin to prove the existence of the resonance.

If we go back to the beginning and understand the specific resonance that we are working with in *Project ONE*, we are working with the feminine resonance. The feminine resonance that lives within the womb space of every female body is moving in a rotational pattern. In the physical body, if observed, the cells are moving in a rotational pattern. Even though they may seem to be moving randomly, there is a rotational pattern that is still occurring. That means that the resonance in the womb space is also moving in this rotational pattern. The feminine resonance, the Divine Mother resonance, is moving in a rotational pattern in the womb. This is all you need to understand: that the feminine resonance is moving in a rotational pattern inside the womb. This is a circular pattern. This is the pattern that is eternal because the circle has no end. This rotational pattern is eternal. This means that the resonance itself is eternal. This is the cycle of eternity. The rotational pattern is the cycle of eternity.

Now you say, "When we die, we die. This is not eternal." Correct. The physical experience is not eternal. The physical experience is a dense experience because of the gravitational pull experienced in the physical life. The experience of the multidimensional human is eternal and never dies. It is always in motion. The universe is eternal. The rotational pattern symbolizes the eternity of the multidimensional universe. Rotational equals eternal. This is what you have to know. Rotational equals eternal.

RECORD 10

ENERGY

What we are going to discuss right now relates to some of your questions about who we are. As we have said before, we are the Higher Force of Collective Consciousness. This is an energetic force—collective consciousness, meaning the collective consciousness of humanity and all that is. It is not just the collective consciousness of humanity. It is the collective consciousness of humanity and all that is.

What this means—this collective consciousness of all that is—is an interdimensional consciousness. It is an interdimensional consciousness of all that is within creation. This is the all. Now, this does not mean God, although God exists in all.

This means that this is the widest consciousness that exists within the collective consciousness. There are many collective consciousnesses. You are creating collective consciousness with everybody you interact with. You have a family collective consciousness. You have the collective consciousness of a school, or work. Humanity has many collective consciousnesses. If you go outside of humanity, there is infinite collective consciousness—infinite collective consciousness in the interdimensional universe. What you can understand is that we are the collective consciousness of all that is.

Now, this sounds ambiguous. What is the higher force of the collective consciousness of all that is? What that means when you say the term *energetic force* is that it is energy in motion. It is conscious beings moving as an energetic force of the collective consciousness through vessels.

Now, this collective consciousness, if you can imagine it, of all that is, is conscious beings. Yes, it is. But it is not entities as you will imagine them to be. Rather, it is consciousness.

RECORD 11

MULTIVERNACULAR ABILITY

What we will be speaking about today is multivernacular ability. Now you ask, what is multivernacular ability? You have to trust the information coming through. This is new information to you that you do not understand. But as we said in the beginning, you will be guided in this process.

Multivernacular ability is one that has been dormant, but it is an ability that every human being possesses and can begin to use at this time.

You ask, "What is multivernacular?" It is the ability to communicate multidimensionally. Now, when we put it into those words, you begin to understand, because you are already beginning to see multidimensionally.

"Why is this important to the feminine resonance theory, and why is it important to *Project ONE*," you ask? The reason why the ability to communicate multidimensionally or to possess multivernacular ability is important is because it supports you in understanding the language of the multidimensional universe. This is a form of telepathic ability.

Now, the ability to speak telepathically and see the multidimensional universe is important for the evolution of humanity. Now, you ask, "Why is this important for accessing God and doing God's work on this earth?"

As you begin to use your multivernacular ability, you can begin to explain more clearly to others what the soul is. Once somebody is able to use this multivernacular ability and is aware of the existence of the multidimensional universe, they can begin to understand the soul.

Once they can begin to understand the soul, they can begin to understand eternal life with God. There *is* an eternal life with God. In the multidimensional universe, this is well known. It is only in this physical plane that this information is questioned by humanity, the question of the existence of God.

So once you begin to use your ability to be a multivernacular human being, to be able to speak telepathically and see within the multidimensional universe, you will be able to clearly see and explain—giving proof to others—that this does exist, that the soul does exist, because the soul is eternal, and the soul is ever present in all the dimensions of the universe at all times. In other dimensions, you step outside of time and space, so you are existing eternally.

Therefore, if you are living eternally in the other dimensions, then you are living eternally in this dimension as well. Now, this is confusing because you say, "Well, I'm born with a body, and my body dies, so how am I living eternally in this dimension?" What we mean to say is that the soul also lives eternally in the physical dimension. The soul is eternal. Everything that exists in the physical dimension exists in the higher dimensions as well. These are like parallel universes. All that exists in this dimension exists in all the other dimensions as well.

So back to your multivernacular ability and why this is important to the feminine resonance project. This is an innate ability that you have in order to begin to prove soul intelligence.

There are many people who are able to see multidimensionally but do not even realize it. As these people come forth, as every person comes forth and begins to document this, the data will be overwhelming. Being able to speak multidimensionally is nothing more than being able to speak telepathically. When you pray, you are speaking multidimensionally and telepathically. That is all this is. What you do not realize is that this is an ability you have—to be able to communicate with others—on this dimension and others.

Now, the fact that you exist in every dimension is very difficult to understand. Since these other dimensions do not include time and space, only the physical plane includes time and space. It only exists in the physical dimension. So, as you exist in the other dimensions, without time and space you exist in the eternal realm. You exist in eternity. As you exist in the eternal realm as of God, you are of God—always in this dimension or any other dimension. It is well known that you are of God in any other dimension. What you do not know is that you are of God in the physical dimension. Now, you do not know that you are of God in the physical dimension because of the density and vibration of the cells that you consist of.

Along with this density and the gravitational pull of the physical world, you are pulled down in this density, and you believe that you are in this physical realm without God. You believe that you are in this physical realm without God because God is a resonance that has no density. You believe yourself to be separate from God because you are a dense human being, and God has no density. The miraculous concept of the human being is that you are made up of many resonances and are a vessel for resonances. This is a miracle of humanity.

As you vibrate with all these various resonances moving through you, you have the ability to access all of this by using this multivernacular ability. Now, you will learn how to use this multivernacular ability over the coming year. You will make great strides in your ability to scientifically prove soul intelligence.

All you need to be concerned about today is knowing that your multivernacular ability will be an important component in the formula for the feminine resonance project. That is all you need to understand today.

This is an ability that you can begin to use now as your cellular data is being reprogramed, as the consistency of what you are made up of is transforming.

RECORD 12

THE FORMULA

As we continue to discuss *Project ONE*, we need to share with you how this formula will be laid out.

First, this formula is working multidimensionally. This formula is energetically coded to transmit energy to those who are working with the formula. Now, the formula is also teaching those to access this energy within themselves. It is an energetically coded formula, but it is also a formula that will teach you how to access the energy within yourselves.

Now, what we mean by energy is the life force within you. It is a divine energy. It is the energetic resonance of God, *ONE*. This formula is coded so that as you begin to engage and work with the formula, you will begin to access this energy. You are not only accessing this energy because you are working with the formula; you are accessing this energy because you are using your Free Will to be able to access it.

The formula is teaching you how to access it as well. So, as we said in the beginning, this is a multidimensional project, and it is a multilayered project with many aspects. This is not a simple project. This is not a simple formula. This is a formula that is quite complicated, working through many dimensions, many universes, and through time and space. What do we mean by working through time and space? This formula is *working* through time and space, meaning that it *bypasses* time and space.

Up to this point, we have discussed components of the formula. There will be more components to the formula than what we have discussed already. How we lay out this formula will be quite important to the trajectory of the work.

Now, once you begin to access the soul intelligence within, you will be working in symbiosis with your soul intelligence to do the work through the process of your life. Your life will be the project. So you ask, "Okay, well, this is the feminine resonance project, which is the female or the feminine energy within the female body. So how will this work for men? How is this possible?"

As the formula is laid out, men will be able to work with this formula with a different resonance, and that will be the *male* feminine resonance. So, men will be working with this formula with the male feminine resonance, and women will be working with this formula with the female feminine resonance.

With regard to gender neutrality, if you do not identify with being a male or a female, that is okay. What you must do is ask yourself what you were when you were born. Whichever gender you were born into scientifically is what you should apply when doing this work. This is not about identity. Identity is held by the ego. Now, you may say, "Well, I was born a male, but I do not identify as being a male." That is okay. There is nothing wrong with that. But you must do the project as if you were in the male body. So, you would apply it to the male feminine resonance within you. This is all you need to know.

We need to lay the groundwork for this formula. First, how will this be effective? You ask, "How long will this formula take to be impactful in my own life?" That is up to each human being. It can work immediately or take years. It depends on the consciousness of each individual, and how much they are willing to use their Free Will to access their soul intelligence to guide them in this process. While time is important to this process, you can rest, knowing that this work is being done.

All we have done thus far is introduce you to the subject matter, to terminology that will be important for the engagement of this work. This terminology will be important for you in order to understand the outcome of this formula. We are now at the beginning, so we can resume the work.

RECORD 13

YOUR ASSIGNMENT

So, what is the topic that we are discussing today?

We have introduced you to the terminology, and now we are going to lay out how this project will unfold and how it will be communicated to others. This project will be communicated to others through various forms. We are just beginning the bulk of the project now.

One component cannot exist without the other component. There will be three major components to this project. All components should be used in symbiosis.

So you say, "There are three components to this project, but this doesn't make sense. What are the three components?" The first component will be the reading material that each person will be given. What we will call the person embarking upon this work is the *sample matter*. The sample matter will need to be able to do the reading material along with dictation that they will have to listen to as well. There will be a dictation, and there will be a reading portion. They will have to do both. They work together. One does not work without the other.

The third component will be the data and the recording. It will be important for the sample matter to record their own progress along with doing this work. It is important for them because they will need to look back and see where they came from and where they are now. This is the data that they will be collecting.

So, one, they will have to listen to dictation. Two, they will have to do the reading work. And three, they will have to collect their own data. This is a project. So as the person embarks upon this work, they are doing an actual project themselves, and they *are* the project themselves.

You ask, "Will they have to turn in this progress?" No, they do not have to turn in the recording. It is going to be for their own information. But it is important that they take the recording because they may not remember everything and how they progress along the way while doing this project.

Again, this is what we have meant by saying that it is a multilayered project: There are many facets to the project for the person embarking upon the work or the sample matter. They will not have to just do reading; they will need to listen to dictation and transmission, and they will need to collect data on their own progress.

As you sit here at the beginning of this project, now you understand the terminology better. Now you understand the goal of the project better. Now you understand how the project will seek to work with each individual. You will need to listen to dictation. You will have reading material. You will need to collect your own data and progress upon doing this work. This will make this project come alive.

What this project is doing is demonstrating the science of humanity and creation to humans. Science can meet with God.

The two go hand in hand. One does not need to exclude the other. Science is a great achievement of humanity. Science would not be without God, because God is all. This you can have faith in.

As you continue to do this project, your faith in God as a species will be a requirement. Now you say, "Science seeks to prove God. How can science have faith in the unknown?"

Science does not need to seek the proof of God. Yes, you need your faith. You need your faith to be able to understand God. This is true. Science seeks to prove humanity more than God, and God lives within humanity. This is what science seeks to prove more than anything. As you make these correlations as a civilization, you will understand the story of creation. This is something you do not understand yet. Although you think you do, you really do not. Once you understand the story of creation, you will be able to understand yourself more and what your intention is here as a species, the species of God.

You are the species of God. You are made in the image and likeness of God. As you begin to understand this, science will validate it back to you. Right now, you are creating a mirror, and science is your mirror. It is your reality in the physical dimension.

As you begin this project, you have to know that there are three components to this project. There will be reading material, there will be dictation that will need to be listened to, and you will need to take data on your own experience with this material.

RECORD 14

YOUR REQUIREMENT

Today we are going to discuss you, the reader, or otherwise we will refer to you as the subject matter—the subject matter being represented by code one. Every human being has the ability to be a subject matter. As we have said in the past, Free Will is a prerequisite for this project. The reason being is once you have begun this project, it is important that you be aligned to truth, and you can only be aligned to truth once you are using your Free Will.

If you have not begun to access your Free Will, than you will not be able to complete the project, as it will simply not work. Therefore, the state of being that you come into this project with is important to the outcome of the project. The other component that will be a requirement from you is that you begin this work with a desire for the outcome of this project to be for the highest good of all humanity.

Therefore, you must be clear within yourself, and your intention to contribute to the higher good of all humanity. This is not only a project of the self, but a collective project. This project is setting a foundation for your collective evolution. As the data is collected from each person or each subject matter, it is important that the intention of the project be done for the highest good of humanity.

For the participatory work, you have now learned to use your Free Will to access your soul intelligence. This is aligning you to truth. It is important to set your intention. This is the next step in the process. You must set your intention for the highest good of humanity.

Please sit at 3:33 and make the intention to call on your soul intelligence to support you in accessing the feminine resonant field. Once you are in that field, you must set the intention that this work will be done for the highest good of humanity. This is an important step in the process. Your intention must be clear that this is being done for the highest good of humanity, as the project is called *Project ONE* so that you can evolve together. Your state of being is a requirement for this work.

Now, let us resume the teaching. Where we left you is being able to access the feminine resonant field and explaining that the resonances work on a wheel or a spectrum. All things carry sound and frequency. It all carries sound, frequency, and color. This is physics, as we have said before. You are made of these resonances. This is why music, the sound, speaks to your soul, because you are comprised of sound.

As you begin accessing the feminine resonant field, sound will play a role. You ask, "How is sound going to be important? Am I supposed to hear anything, and what is it that I'm supposed to hear?"

Yes! Do not become alarmed if you do not hear anything. However, chances are that you will hear something as you do this work with time. You will hear a high-pitched tone when you are in the feminine resonance field. Once you hear a high-pitched tone, you can know this to be true.

Now, if you are doing the participatory work and you expect a certain outcome, then it will not be because you are setting expectations. Do not set any expectations. Just know as you access this feminine resonant field that you will begin to hear higher tones that will become more distinguished in your hearing. This is nothing more than the resonant field becoming more clear. This is the resonance energy. The reason why it becomes more clear *around* you is because it is becoming more clear *within* you.

Know that sound itself today has become distorted from the divine. Sound has become muffled, the reason being that you are not hearing clearly. Once you begin to hear clearly, sound will emerge as something different from what you have known it to be.

Gradients of sounds will become more pronounced. This is nothing more than the higher resonances becoming more clear. Now, you say,

"Why are we talking about all higher resonances? I thought we were just talking about the feminine resonance."

For now we are just discussing the feminine resonance. But the higher resonances will become more clear as you begin to do this work. Yes, you will begin to hear sounds in a more pronounced way, and some of those who have had awakenings understand what this is, because in the awakening process, sounds become more distinct and distinguished, and you can hear them in a more pronounced way. Remember, you are all made of sound, color, and frequency. This is energy.

We would like you to sit in the feminine resonant field. Again, please set the intention that this be for the highest good of humanity. The next step as you are sitting in the field is to please ask for the support of God to make the feminine resonance clear.

You have now used your Free Will to work with your soul intelligence and God to be able to make the feminine resonance clear. As you do this, please sit and notice and pay attention to what is happening within this field. You are now transforming the energy within you as you begin to do this. As you begin to transform the energy, you will feel more expansion within your body.

As you begin to transform the feminine resonance field, you will experience light within your entire body. The feminine resonance holds an infinite amount of light, which holds a high-pitched, clear tone. You may hear differently, but you will also *feel* differently. You will feel a lighter energy inside you that will permeate throughout your body as it permeates the other resonances.

So, what you are going to do today, and *all* you are going to do today is set the intention that this work be done for the highest good of humanity, and simply ask God to begin to clear the resonance. Now, clearing the resonance means to make the resonance clear. Clear color, clear sound. That is what clearing the resonance is.

RECORD 15

THE LAW OF THE MULTIDIMENSIONAL UNIVERSE

What is the topic today? We will continue to discuss the feminine resonance field, and your participatory work within the field.

The feminine resonance lives inside you, but it is also an energetic field that you can access in the multidimensional universe. The energetic resonances that live inside you exist within the universe as fields. You have not been able to quantify fields by science; therefore, there is a misinterpretation of what a field is. However, an energetic field has the potential to be quantified by science.

With this work, you have begun to access the energetic field. What do you do once you are in the field? You know what it is now to be in the field, and you may even feel a shift. However, you will be learning how to navigate and operate in this space.

You are calling upon the multidimensional self within you, or your soul intelligence. Your soul intelligence itself is helping you access the energy field, and that is what is bringing you to the energy field. The multidimensional self is accessing the energy field, not you.

As you are accessing this energy field, what do you do once you are in the energy field itself? Know that this energy field is not detectable to the human eye; it is only detectable to the multidimensional self. This is the prerequisite that we have been discussing up until this point. However, once you have accessed the field with the multidimensional self, you will experience change within the physical self.

You ask, "How is it possible that I access an energetic field with the multidimensional self, but I noticed the shift in the physical self and I can't access it with the physical self?"

This is a law of the universe, and it works like this: Your Free Will is of the physical self. Your soul intelligence is of the multidimensional self. You can access other dimensions with the multidimensional self. You cannot access other dimensions with the physical self. However, these other dimensions can access the physical universe; therefore, you will see the impact within the physical self or your physical reality.

This is how it works. This is a law. The multidimensional component within you can access the multidimensional universe. The physical self cannot. The physical self must use Free Will, which is a gift of your life to access the multidimensional self, which can access the multidimensional universe. The multidimensional universe can then access the physical self. This is a possibility. When you make change in the multidimensional universe, you will see the reflection back in the physical landscape. This is the bridge between science and spirituality.

Up until now, science has been of the physical landscape. It has not accessed the multidimensional landscape. It has only been of the physical landscape. You need the multidimensional self to be able to bridge science and spirituality, which is the multidimensional universe, the multidimensional self. This is what you have not had.

So here you are. You have now used your Free Will to access the multidimensional component within you to be able to access the energetic field that exists in the multidimensional universe. You are in this field.

Now you will empower this field through conscious Free Will, again. As you empower this energetic field, the energetic field expands. That is what is going to be happening in this project.

So for today, we only ask that you do the following: Please become comfortable with simply sitting in the energetic field. Acclimate to how it feels as you sit in this space. You will be doing work in this space, but first become comfortable with accessing and sitting within the space. This is a large step for you. Sitting in the space and acclimating to this energy will bring you confidence and trust.

Today, as you sit and acclimate to this space, please know that the component of God can work with you now. Through God, you will be able to empower this energy field itself. This will, in turn, be reflected back to you in your physical life, because as we have said, the multidimensional universe can access the physical universe.

You have now made the intention that this work will be done for the highest good of humanity. This has been the intention that you have made. And now, as you sit in this field and you have accessed this field, you have to call upon the energy of love and God to work through you as you are sitting in this field.

You are a vessel of God in action. You are made in the image and likeness of God. You have denied God for so long within you that this energy has been distorted. As you begin to empower it again through your realignment to God, you will see your physical composition begin to change.

You will be able to document and have data to show you what this physical shift will be. This is the process, and this is happening now.

Today, please remember to document your session in the feminine resonance field.

RECORD 16
CELLULAR DATA

What is the topic today?

We have now introduced you to the participatory work of being able to access the energetic field with your soul intelligence. The next step in this process is to work with your cellular data.

You ask, "What is cellular data, exactly?" Cellular data is composed of matter that is detectable to the human eye. Just like anything else in the universe, it is also composed of matter that is not detectable to the human eye. This is the matter that exists in the multidimensional universe. A cell is composed of physical matter and multidimensional matter as well. The multidimensional matter within the cell is the matter of the energetic field.

The cell carries data within it. This is the cellular data that you have been born into through lineage. Cellular data exists in the physical dimension, otherwise known as DNA, and in the multidimension. The cellular data that exists within the physical dimension is giving you clear information as to your genetic predisposition.

Science has been able to study this, and understand genetics to a great extent. However, there is a multidimensional aspect of the cellular data. This is where the energetic field comes into play.

Similar to how you know that cells have been distorted in the physical landscape, cells are also distorted in the multidimensional landscape. You bring the cells to wholeness once you do this work. The multidimensional cellular data will be altered within you to be reflected back in your physical body. This is the bridge between spirituality and science.

Soul intelligence is the bridge to link science and spirituality. You alter your physical self through working within the multidimensional fields.

It is your responsibility to document this work so that it can be useful to prove to humankind the use of soul intelligence for the betterment of humanity. You will be able to use this to advance your scientific technologies.

For today, as you embark upon 3:33, we ask you to sit in the energetic field of the feminine resonance. All we want you to do is shift into that and sit in that space within you today, and notice that this is inside you.

RECORD 17

A DISCLAIMER

As you, the reader, embark upon this project, there is a disclaimer. "What is that disclaimer?" you ask. This disclaimer is that anything that happens in this project, anything that happens as a result of this project, is a result of your own Free Will. This is on your behalf. Nobody is doing this to you. The reason why we are making this disclaimer is because it is important for you to know that any kind of healing work is not happening *to* you from another person or source. Rather, we are guiding you to see that *you* are the true healer of yourself. You are your own master. You work with God. This is the disclaimer.

Now, back to *Project ONE*. We are discussing the faith in God itself, the actual energy of faith itself.

As you begin this work and as you sit in the feminine resonance field, you must have faith in God. Now you say, "Faith is the antithesis to science. It's not science. So how is this possible? Why are you asking us to have faith and trust when that is not scientifically proven?"

This is why. Once you have added faith into this equation, and in the end result, there is enough actual physical data, you will understand that faith can be proven scientifically through data and documentation. The only way that it can be proven is actual evidence, actual proof of people who have come together to be able to do this work and experience an actual shift in the physical landscape. This is not stuff formed in the clouds. This is grounded. It is going to make a change in your physical landscape and in your physical body as well.

As we discussed the laws prior, the law of the multidimensional and physical universe, we discussed that any work done in the multidimensional universe can be reflected back in the physical universe. This is what you will be doing. For this to work, you must have faith.

As you sit in the feminine resonance field and you have accessed it, you have made the intention that this is for the highest good of humanity.

Now, you can call upon God with faith. In this process, you are empowering the feminine resonant field itself. Once you empower the feminine resonant field, the other energies will become compliant. Right now, the feminine resonance field has been overwrought by aggressive energies because it is a peaceful energy. As the feminine becomes more powerful, the dominant energies will dissipate. This is the process, and it is all happening within your cells.

All you need to do is sit and ask God to help the healing of the feminine resonance within you. That is all you need to do. You must have faith and trust in that process. As more data is collected over time, the doubts and hesitations will begin to dissipate.

You are the pioneers of this work, and as the pioneers, it is required that you have significant trust in this work. This is a requirement, but you will see the reflection back in your physical landscape.

Now, all we are going to ask for you to do today is sit with this state, the state of being in the feminine resonance field. So now at 3:33 today, you have accessed the feminine resonant field, through God and your own Free Will, with your soul intelligence. Once you have accessed this state, once you have accessed this field, you can go in and understand that your soul intelligence is working with you to actually heal this field, and that your soul intelligence is working with you to heal this field within you and around you. This is happening now at a multidimensional level. That is how this is working. That is why we said when we started this project that this is a multilayered project and a multidimensional project.

You are actually working in a multidimensional universe now. You have been brought from not understanding what this project would be at all to now sitting in the multidimensional universe and working within that multidimensional universe with soul intelligence and God. You have come quite a long way in a very short amount of time. So now as you are working in this process, as you are working in this state, as you are working in the feminine resonance field, you need to hand it over to God. As you hand it over to God, say, "God, I have trust and faith that you are healing the feminine resonant field within me and around me in the multidimensional universe."

You are empowering the feminine resonant field in itself. Do this every day, and record what you experience after you do it. We are going to leave it at that right now. As you embark upon this state of being, you can find peace in the state of being. This is all you need to do for today.

RECORD 18

THE BODY

What are we going to be discussing today? The body and consumption. This is an important topic as far as where humanity is going. Consumption is important for the evolution of humanity.

You all consume too much. This you know to be true, but what you do not understand is the reason why you consume too much. Energetically, you are experiencing such large distortions within you, individually and collectively, that you are not in balance or aligned to what your needs are. Therefore, you do not know what your needs are, so you consume in an attempt to fill those needs.

When you fall into limitation, you begin to overconsume what you do not need or what is not required for you. You must become realigned with the needs that you require as a species to consume in order to move forward.

There is resurgence in the health of the physical body. This is important to the evolution of humanity. But what you do not realize is that while you are all focused on the health and wellness of what you take in, you are still not understanding that you are taking in too much.

As you continue to overconsume, you continue the patterning of the distorted physical body. In the physical universe, if you do not have awareness of what is happening, you will continue to revert to old patterns because this has been programmed into your DNA.

As you begin to do this work, you are reprogramming your actual cellular data. You must continue to do the work every day in order to see an impact. As the cellular data shifts, you will see your needs change. When you notice that your physical needs change, you must follow that. You must listen to that. You must move forward with the changes of your physical body, because as your physical body changes, you will shift energetically as well. You work in symbiosis. The physical universe works in symbiosis with the multidimensional universe.

Now, you ask, what are the physical changes that you will begin to see? You will see many physical changes, and you will feel them immediately. However, you must do this every day. You must do the meditation every day in order for it to be effective, because your body is acclimating to this energy. As you, the reader, embark upon this work, your body is acclimating to this energy or to this frequency. As you acclimate to this energy, you begin to get momentum toward your healing of the individual resonances within you. As you get momentum toward the healing, you need to continue that momentum.

So what we ask is that you sit in the energy today. As you sit in the energy, begin to take notice of what happens in your physical body. You will begin to see the shifts immediately. Allow yourself to record the data and document what those shifts are. As you record the data and document what the shifts are, you will begin to see new patterns emerging. This will not happen overnight. The new patterns will emerge over time. So today, all we ask is that you sit in the energy and allow yourself to simply feel this and acclimate to it. That is all you need to do today.

RECORD 19
SOUL INTELLIGENCE

What will we be discussing today? Soul intelligence.

You have learned that soul intelligence is a component that does have intelligence that exists within the soul, but you still ask, "What is soul intelligence, exactly? Is this my higher self?"

Soul intelligence is a component of the higher self. It is not the higher self in the entirety of the higher self. Rather, it is a component of the higher self.

Soul intelligence specifically gives you the knowledge that you need to be able to move forward. It is the aspect of the soul that holds data and memory. Your soul intelligence actually holds memory within a memory bank. You can consider it the record keeper of the soul. It contains all of the data that your soul has ever experienced and ever will experience in that data record keeper. It exists within that record keeper. This is what the soul intelligence actually is itself.

Now the reason why you are working with soul intelligence specifically in this project is because the work that you are going to be doing in the multidimensional universe will require you to work with your soul intelligence because it holds all the data that your soul has ever experienced. It is the record keeper of the soul. As the record keeper of the soul, it carries every experience of your soul. Therefore, it is important that you call on your soul intelligence when you are correcting distortions of the resonance field.

Let us go into the work now. Today, as you are sitting in this exercise we are guiding you through, the first step is to call on your soul intelligence. As you do this, please do not worry about your past. You do not need to look at any trauma, or question any trauma of the past. Your soul intelligence will rectify the past for you.

Allow your soul intelligence to guide you through the process of the reconciliation of all records of your soul. This is what the soul intelligence will do.

Soul intelligence has a collective soul as well. You will first be working with the soul intelligence of your individual self in *Project ONE*. However, there is a collective soul intelligence for all of humanity that holds all records of the collective soul of humanity. This will eventually be worked with to be able to correct any distortions.

As the record keeper of your soul, this is the component that holds all data that your soul has ever experienced. There is nothing that is imperfect in the eyes of God. It is all-perfect in God's eyes. As you are doing this work, please know that any distortion is already perfect in the eyes of God.

Please become committed to doing this exercise every day. As you commit to this practice, you will begin to see alterations in your physical reality. You will also collect data for yourself about this experience. As you begin to access the higher dimensions, your soul intelligence will also be keeping a record as well. This will bring the resonant field into balance.

What you need to do is empower your soul intelligence to be able to go through the records of your soul and bring this database into balance. Now you ask, "How is this possible if, in the eyes of God, my soul is already perfect?" The database of your soul intelligence contains faulty records. You are going to go back to these faulty records and begin to reconcile the faulty records. However, you are not the one who is going to be doing this; rather, your soul intelligence will be doing this.

When you do this exercise today, sit and access your soul intelligence. As you go through the protocol of sitting in the feminine resonant field, please ask your soul intelligence to restore all the records of the database within your soul, and to bring any faulty records to healing. This is all you need to do today—just this one step.

RECORD 20

WORKING WITH GOD

What is the topic today, you ask? This is about the feminine resonance.

The feminine resonance itself, as you know it to be, is an energetic field. It is the field that you are accessing as you do the exercises given to you. As you are accessing this field, you are empowering it back to wholeness.

We are choosing the feminine resonant field first, because as it becomes balanced, all other fields can become balanced much quicker. The feminine resonance field was created during creation itself. One resonance was existed at the time of creation. Thereafter, more resonances were created from that one resonance.

This is how your soul was conceived. The soul was created through these energetic resonances. Because of this, these energetic resonances still live within you, and exist in the multidimensional universe. These energetic resonances that your soul was conceived from are carried with you through lifetimes. They are of creation.

All of life is created from these resonances. The feminine resonance was here during creation, and is perfect. It is only distorted in the physical plane among human physical beings. It is only distorted in the physical universe.

When you are doing this work in the higher dimension, you are working with a perfect feminine resonance. As you work with that resonance, you can make it whole in the physical field as well. You are working in the parallel universe to impact the physical universe. You will find that the resonance itself becomes clear and perfect in the physical universe.

As you access this higher dimension, you are working with a perfect resonant field. As you work within the perfect resonant field, you are empowering it, and you can hand any healing work over to God. You will begin to heal it on the physical plane, as any work you do on the higher dimension directly impacts the physical dimension.

Through Free Will and God, you are accessing the perfect feminine resonance at 3:33 with your soul intelligence. You hand the healing of the field to God, while embodying this perfect state. As you do this, you transform the cells within you in the physical dimension to that perfected state. This is what is happening. You are shifting the cellular structure within your physical body on the physical plane. You are now changing cellular data.

And as you do it every day, you will begin to see it reflected back to you. Now you need to continue to do this and use the data and documentation to record.

So today, what we ask you to do is sit in the feminine resonant field again. Hand over the field to God. As you bring and embody this state into your physical body, you will begin to see the healing occur. This is because you are embodying the perfect feminine resonant field that exists in the higher dimension. You are bringing it into the physical dimension now. This is what you are doing.

RECORD 21

A COMPILATION

What are we going to be discussing in *Project ONE* today? We are going to be discussing a compilation.

A compilation is something that is composed of many components. So you could say that there is a compilation of music, there is a compilation of sound, there is a compilation of art. You could have a compilation of many things, but we are going to be discussing a compilation of frequency.

As we have discussed before, a resonance itself contains many chords. These chords make up the resonance. And then, there can be many resonances—many resonances that make up a compilation, a compilation of resonances. Now, why we are discussing the compilation of resonances is because there is an entire resonance system for you to learn.

As we discussed previously, creation began with only three resonances. From those three resonances, many resonances split off, and there existed many more resonances. There is a compilation of resonances within each person. This compilation of resonances makes up the entirety of who you are, and each resonance is a component of the entire compilation.

This system works much like sound. Each vibration, or each note, makes up the entire sound. Each fragment of sound makes up the entirety of its sound. The fragment of a resonance makes up the entirety of the resonance. The fragment of the resonance is its chord. The entire resonance is the resonance. And then, when many resonances come together, it is a compilation of resonances. This is what we are going to be discussing today.

So as we are talking about the compilation of resonances, there are many unique compilations. In fact, there are infinite resonances, just as there are infinite sounds. These resonances exist in all dimensions, including the physical dimension. This is because of the original three resonances that existed after creation, from these resonances every resonance was made. So as you understand everything to be made in the image and likeness of God, it is true because it is from God that everything was made. And the original resonance, the first resonance of creation, was the resonance of God. Everything was made from this resonance.

God was the first resonance within all resonances, even though every resonance is unique. That is what we are going to be discussing throughout *Project ONE*.

Now, why do you need to know this for *Project ONE*? Why do you need to understand the compilation of resonances? While you are working with the feminine resonance, it is important to understand that every other resonance is important to the entirety of who you are. There should be no resonance that is dismissed, as every resonance itself is important to the entire compilation. Every resonance includes God. Even the lowest resonances are of God and are created from the resonance of God itself.

God was a resonance, and everything came from that resonance. The first three resonances were the feminine resonance, the masculine resonance, and the *ONE* resonance of God. Everything stemmed from these three resonances, therefore exists within *ALL*.

RECORD 22

THE RESONANCE SYSTEM

What will we be discussing today, you ask? The entirety of the resonance system and collective humanity.

For each resonance to be in balance, the compilation in its entirety must be in balance similar to an ecosystem. The totality of all resonances is important to each resonance. This applies to humanity as well. Each human being's evolution is critical for the healing and evolution of the collective totality of all human beings.

You cannot evolve while another is left behind. It is not possible. All human beings are entitled to the embodiment of the higher self. Now, you ask, "How is this possible? So I cannot become whole as long as another is not?" Yes, this is true. You cannot fully embody the liberated self until you have all been liberated.

Now, what does this mean? This means that this is a collective process. You are all made in the image and likeness of God. The collective healing of humanity is important to individual healing as well. Now, when we say the word *healing*, all we mean is that the distortion that has happened to humanity is corrected or put into balance again.

As we are working with the feminine resonance during this project, other resonances will soon be brought into balance as well. However, we are just focusing on the feminine resonance for this project.

At the end of *Project ONE*, you will see how the formula is working. We have discussed many components of the formula, and we have taken you through exercises to show you how this works.

You have the subject matter. You have your Free Will. You have your soul intelligence. You have God. You have all of the other components of the feminine resonance. You have the actual feminine resonance itself. You have sound. You have rotational motion. You have the physics of the resonance theory itself.

This formula is energetically coded, so it is important that this formula be laid out very carefully.

The end result of the formula will be the evolved human being embodying God, the higher self. The formula is being created in conjunction with the project; therefore, it is experiential. You must experience this work as you participate.

Now, as we move forward in this formula, you will be accountable for participating in the project. You will be accountable for doing the homework from this day forward.

RECORD 23
ASSISTANT ENERGY

What will we be discussing today? A new energy that has emerged called the *assisting energy*.

As you now know, the resonance system began with one resonance, and from there, three resonances formed. The new energy coming into the planet today is of God, as all resonances; however, there is a different equation making up the subsistence of this energy. Much like colors on a color wheel, there is white and black. All color derives from white, and black is the absence of color. This is how the resonance system works.

There is now a new resonance that has been created from the energetic resonance of God to be able to help lift the planet.

Why is this relevant to the feminine resonance project? This energy is going to assist you, and that is why this energy is here for you today. This is the next component of the equation that is going to be very important to the feminine resonance project. So far, through this project, you have learned how to access the feminine resonance and to sit within this space using your soul intelligence and Free Will.

Now we are moving into the next part of this project where you will use this new energy on the planet. This new energy that seeks to come into the planet is using the human body to be anchored into the planet. The human body is a vessel for this assisting energy. It is here to assist; therefore, it is called the assisting energy. That is what it is here to do.

RECORD 24

THE HARMONY OF THE RESONANCE SYSTEM

What will we be discussing today? The harmony of the resonance system. What do we mean by the word *harmony*?

You are now learning about the foundational concepts of the resonance system and how it works. This is an introduction. To understand these concepts is beneficial for your greater healing. First, you have many resonances, and these resonances work together to provide balance to the universe in the physical dimension and the multidimensional space.

All resonances work together; therefore, there is not one resonance that is excluded from the entirety of all resonances. Now you ask, "How is this possible?" As we have spoken about before, the resonances exist on a spectrum, much like a color wheel.

When you were born into this world, into the physical dimension, you brought with you a set of experiences that were carried within the soul—specifically, soul intelligence. You were also born into this world as a vessel of your unique energetic resonance system.

This system operates within you and all throughout creation. You are the unique carrier of this energetic system. This system is being reflected back to you in this physical life as who you are. The physical dimension is nothing more than a mirror for this energetic system.

In the higher dimensions, you do not have this mirror. It is not needed in the higher dimensions because you specifically come into the physical world for the experience of expansion. In higher dimensions, you do not need to go through the process of expansion. You are already expanded.

In the physical dimension, you experience form. In this form you are the vessel for your energetic system. This system does exist in the higher dimensions along with your soul.

When you are born into this physical dimension with your soul and energetic system, know that your soul is a fixed constant, while your resonance system is always in motion. The energetic system shifts. So, while your soul is always constant, the energetic system is always in motion. When the universe was created with one resonance, there were resonances that were created from that one resonance because the energetic system is always in motion. Energy is always moving.

Throughout time, this brought about confusion when it came to studies of the soul, because how is it possible if your consciousness is always in evolution but your soul is always present in the now? This is because your soul is always constant, throughout time into the now. However, the energetic system is always changing and always shifting.

Returning to the harmony of the resonance system, the system must work together in order to be in balance. It is a matter of how you are working with the system to be in balance. This is the trick.

To expand into the higher state, which you have the ability to do, you must work with the entire energetic system. This is key. Now, specifically in *Project ONE*, we are talking about the feminine resonance. We will continue to go back to the feminine resonance throughout this project. Once we have gone through the feminine resonance, we will be layering up additional resonances, and you will begin to see how these resonances interact with each other.

Now you ask, "How is it possible that the energetic system is distorted if everything is made in the image and likeness of God?" The energetic system is not distorted in the higher dimensions. The energetic system is only distorted in the physical dimension. Because when you choose to come into the physical dimension, you are simply choosing to access a parallel universe. That is all you are doing. This is actually nothing more than science. You are choosing to be born into a parallel universe as a human being.

Now you say, "Okay. This is confusing. How does the energetic system shift from one dimension to the next?"

When you are born into the physical dimension, the energetic system shifts. The reason the energetic system shifts is because of the limitation you hold in the physical dimension. This is the key component. The limitation that you have held yourself in is in the physical dimension.

You did not always hold yourself in this limitation in the physical dimension, but you have had to go through this process of limitation. This limitation has been nothing more than a simple construct that has been programmed again in your cellular DNA, as we described when introducing *Project ONE*.

This program does not exist in the higher dimensions. That is why we are teaching you how to access your soul intelligence: because your soul intelligence will do the work for you to be reflected back in the physical dimension. You will be unlocking codes to access each resonant field with your soul intelligence to do healing work in the higher dimension. This work will be reflected back in the physical dimension. You will become more comfortable with this as you begin the work.

Now, what does it mean to see this shift in your physical life? You will be a vessel. Yes, you will. But what you will see is that the resonance system will begin to work in harmony because you will be unlocking limitations that have been held in in your cellular DNA.

As you begin to unlock the limitations that you have held in, you will again restore harmony to this resonance system. This is the harmony of the resonance system.

PART THREE
THE EXPERIMENT

RECORD 25
THE FIELD

What will we be discussing today? We are beginning the experiment.

We have already brought you into the feminine resonance field. This next section will be much more interactive than the first half of the project. You have simply been a passerby sitting in the field. Now you will be interacting with the field itself to be able to work in the field.

This will be experiential work because you will be experiencing it as you are doing it. This work will be for the highest good of all humanity. You are not only doing this work for yourself; you are doing this work for the collective group of humanity.

We have reviewed many components up to this point. Now, during this experiment, you are the sample matter, but you will also be working in groups. Yes, you will be working with each other in groups. It will be important to work in groups because you will see the impact you make for the collective. With this, you can begin to understand the massive change you can make to society at large with this work.

So you will begin doing this work in groups, and the groups will be organized for you. Now, you may be working with a partner on this, you may be working with several partners on this, or you may be working in a large group, but this will be done in groups so that you can see not only the change in the individual self but the change in the collective group as well.

As we begin part 3, please know that as you begin working with your group or your partner, that you will begin to notice what you are as a collective group, whether it be two or fifty people. You will begin to understand what you are as a collective group. Now you say, "Okay, I am doing this all by myself. So how do I do this if I don't have a partner? And is it possible for me to do this if I don't have a partner?"

Yes, it is possible for you to do this if you do not have a partner. All you need to do is request that, and you will be assigned a partner. This will happen. You can request a partner in the higher dimensional space, and you will be assigned a partner that you will be able to work with. This is what you will see begin to happen and unfold in a way that you do not understand, but this is the intention of the work.

The intention of the work is to be able to show you how you can create change in your society. The idea is to gather resources to move you forward as a species. Therefore, doing the work as a collective group will support you in this process. You are no longer in the process of evolution where you are working for yourself. Your evolution is not about the individual alone anymore. This is about evolving through each other. We have stressed that there is not one channel bringing forth this information anymore. There are *many* channels bringing this information through right now. This will be a collective movement forward.

This is not just for the select few. Rather, this is a collective leap forward in humanity. So, it is important for you to understand that you will be doing the work more than for yourself alone. Rather, you are doing this work for humanity.

Up to this point, you have been able to sit in the feminine resonance field, anchoring the perfect feminine resonance into your physical reality. As you make change from this space, you impact your physical reality.

Now you are being asked to work with a partner or group. It can be any partner you feel inclined to work with. If you do not have a partner, please request one.

We are not going to introduce any more than this today because we want you to sit with this. Begin reflecting on how that changes your landscape from being just an individual to a collective group. You may realize that while the collective is different from the individual, it is just as important to your individual evolution.

As you do this work, you will begin to see the change reflected back in your physical landscape. So for today, and today only, we want you to sit and just reflect on this. Reflect back on what it will be like to be an individual working in the feminine resonance field versus working with a partner in the feminine resonance field.

RECORD 26

COLLECTIVE SPECIES

What will we be discussing today? We have discussed doing this work as a collective group, in partnership. The work will be important to do as a collective because as a species, you are moving into a new phase of your evolution. When you think of this new phase of your evolution, you are a collective species. Now, this means that the boundaries you have imposed upon yourself in the form of gender, race, ethnicity, and religion will dissipate. They will dissipate as you move forward as a collective species.

As you move forward as a collective species, it is a requirement that the work of the soul be done through each other. The concept of doing this work as an individual will no longer serve you. Now you are being asked to put another before yourself. As you place another person before yourself, you will expand. This is collective evolution.

Now that you are doing the work in partnership or as a collective group and as you bring forth this initiative to others, they will be able to do this work as well, and the collective grows. Now, as you do this work in collective partnership, you are going to move into the next phase. As we have said before, part 3 is going to be highly experiential. You will be gaining the experience of *Project ONE* more than in the previous sections.

We have been introducing the topic, terminology, and components of the formula so that you can understand how the resonance system works. Now you are moving into the experiential portion of *Project ONE*.

As you begin to access the feminine resonance field each day at 3:33, and are now working with a partner or group, we are going to ask you to extend it further. You have now become acclimated to being able to sit in the resonance field. Your soul intelligence has guided you. You now know what it is to sit in that space and to be able to work with a partner or group. The next step as you are working with your partner is to shift your focus to their healing.

As we have discussed before, the resonance field is similar to a color wheel. This is physics. This is how color works. This is also how resonance works. The color of the resonance that you are specifically working with in *Project ONE* has been dominated by aggressive resonances.

You are empowering the resonance so that it can claim itself again. Through this, the other resonances will become less dominant. You can only empower it through embodying it. That is all that you need to do: embody the resonance in its perfect state.

As you embody the resonance, that resonance is given power. That resonance is empowered to be able to become its true self again. It becomes clear. As you embody that in the higher dimension, you will begin to embody it in your cellular structure in the physical dimension as well.

So now, going back to the exercise at hand and what you need to do to elaborate on in order to experience this project. ... As you are sitting in the resonant field at 3:33 or the next time you choose to sit in the resonant field with your partner or with your group, however it may be, what you have to do is not only surrender the healing of the resonant field to God, but you are going to have to shift your consciousness within the resonance field itself. As you shift your consciousness in the resonance field, you will be able to shift the resonance field itself.

God is going to be working with you on this, as well as your soul intelligence. You will just shift your consciousness within the resonance field. Now, what does this mean, and how do you need to shift your consciousness?

Please see your partner in a perfectly healed state. This is what needs to happen. When you see your partner in the perfectly healed state and you are holding your partner in a state of love, you will embody the resonance in your body. You are projecting outward a state of being that is allowing you to access the perfect energetic field.

Right now what you are doing is simply sitting in the energetic field. But next, you need to embody the resonant field within your body. You embody the resonance in your cells by intending it to be so and projecting it outward toward your partner or group. That is all you need to do: simply intend and allow.

The next time you are sitting in the feminine resonant field, rather than just accessing the higher dimension, you need to ground the higher dimension into you. This is working in symbiosis with the dimensions. Again, how you embody that resonant field into you is simply by intending it to be so. That is all you need to do.

So today or tomorrow when you are sitting in the resonant field, please go through the protocol that is being given to you here. Your next step is setting the intention to ground the resonance field in its perfect state into your physical cellular structure. That is the next intention that you need to do as you are sitting in the resonant field.

As you do that, what you need to do next is simply take data and documentation of what you experience. After you do this, you need to continue to take data and documentation of your physical experiences as you do this work. This work is going to be important because of the data and documentation that you are collecting as a species.

This is a project where you are collecting data and documentation. As you gather documentation from all the people who are going to be able to do this work, you will be able to prove a theory. What that theory is, is simply being able to access the higher dimension and doing the work in the higher dimension and seeing that shift your reality back in the physical dimension. It is a very simple theory. As you prove that theory, you will be able to do it as a collective species, and you will be able to change your physical landscape as a collective species to a vast degree.

RECORD 27

YOUR CATALYST

We will continue to outline your next steps for working in the field.

As we said when we left off, you are to sit in the space to access the higher field. We brought you into working with a partner or group. Now we are bringing you into an interactive role within the resonant field.

In this interactive role within the resonant field, you will be working with the energy to impact your cellular data. How do you begin using it to impact your cellular data? When we began *Project ONE*, we spoke of codes and programs running in your cellular data.

You have now used codes to be able to access the feminine resonant field, and you are using the field to access your cellular data. You have surrendered the healing of the feminine resonance to God. You must have faith in God in the process of this. God is a resonance that lives within you, and you cannot take that away. It is impossible. As we said before, God is a fixed variable in this formula.

As you become acquainted with the higher dimensional space, you will see the impact on your physical body. The cellular data that lives within you is physical. Your cells are of the physical plane. Through the Law of the Multidimensional Universe, the healing work that you do within the higher dimension will be impacting your cellular structure in the physical dimension. So *how* do we affect that cellular structure, and *why* do we want to impact that cellular structure?

First, we must go back to the programs that are within the cellular structure. These programs have made it difficult for you to use your Free

Will. Many of you want to use your own Free Will. Many of you say you are making the right choice. However, you return again to making a choice that is not for your highest good. You do this repeatedly, and the creation becomes embedded into who you are until you actually believe that this is your truth.

This is how you function. Now, how you want to transform the cellular structure is to lift the limitations that have been placed. You want to transform the programming. How you lift the limitations and change the programming is simply through consciousness. There is no other way. There is no other way other than consciousness.

Many of you have begun to transform your cellular structure through consciousness, and this is something that science has begun to study through the use of positive words, words that mean something from a positive place, and using ideas and concepts where you can change your environment to impact your mood. This is slowly transforming your cellular structure.

However, there is a way that you can do this much faster and much more efficiently, and this is from the higher dimensional space. Once you begin to access the higher dimensional space, you can shift the cellular structure rather quickly. When you do that, you will find yourself having a much easier time making choices that are aligned with your greatest good. You will find that you will no longer fall back into old patterns.

Now that you have begun to access the space with your partner or with your group, you are going to be engaging in a more interactive process. This interactive process is going to require, yes, a shift of consciousness. Yes, it is. It is going to require your partner to support you in this process. You will need to rely on your partner and your group in this process because it is through working with other human beings that you can begin to heal yourself. You can go through the process of healing yourself alone, but when you work as a team, it will accelerate the process because you are amplifying the energy as a team.

As you work as a team, you will begin to see the reflection on your cellular structure. So again, we are going to take this step by step. For today and today only, the first step we want you to do is, the next time that you are sitting in the feminine resonant field at 3:33, or the next day that you are sitting in the feminine resonant field with your partner, we are going to ask you to see your partner as healed. Yes, that is part of this work. However, we are going to ask you to take it a step further. What we want you to do in this field is for you and your partner to acknowledge what has happened up until this point to bring you to this place.

The question you must both ask yourselves is, "What brought me to doing this work?" The answers will be quite different for every person; however, they will also be revealing. They are going to be unique for every single person, but they are going to reveal something about yourself. They are going to reveal where the programs have been running in your cellular structure. The work has actually been encoded. The work has been encoded itself to be able to show you this, so as you are doing this work, you will see clearly where the programs have been embedded in you. Please ask yourself, "What has brought me to this place to do this work?" This is your *catalyst*. The answer will reveal your *program*.

Now, you may say, "I don't know what brought me to this place." This could be very true for many people. They may not understand what has brought them into this space. If this is the case, sit for two minutes, call on your soul intelligence, and reflect in silence. The answers will come rather quickly to you.

For each of you, what has brought you to this space is going to reveal where your programs are running inside your cellular structure. Once you have that answer, you can simply use that as your platform to shift your cellular structure. It is going to be unique for each person, as each person is unique in this process.

Now, this answer that you arrived at as to what brought you to doing this work, or the need to do this work, is what we are going to call your catalyst. The channel is asking what has brought her to do this work. Her catalyst is actually an issue she has had for a long time, where she prayed for help with being healed. Now that issue in itself is her catalyst. The program is Obsessive Compulsive Disorder, and that has been her operating system.

It is the program itself that is running within her that needs to be transformed. She can use this as her platform as she embarks into changing her cellular structure. This is where she is going to see the greatest healing as she moves forward in this work. That is all.

RECORD 28

YOUR PROGRAM

We left off in the experiential part of this process. You have become more interactive with transforming cellular data. How you will begin to do that is by navigating the cellular structure and the programs within you by first identifying your catalyst itself.

The catalyst is going to reveal to you what your program is that has been running through you and that has been running through your cellular structure. The catalyst itself is going to be very important to the outcome of this project. You have all been instructed to sit within the resonance field itself and to identify your catalyst. Everybody will have a unique answer to this question.

You may now begin to work with your catalyst. You do not need to go deeply into the catalyst itself, because that is all it is. It is nothing more than a catalyst to be able to throttle you forward into healing the programs within your cellular structure that have been holding you in limitation from being able to expand or hold these higher resonances.

What you have to understand about the programs that have been running through you via the catalyst itself is that the catalyst itself is not the actual program. This is something you need to be clear about. The catalyst itself is nothing more than a manifestation of the program. It can, though, help reveal to you how to dismantle the program within you. Now, the code that you have been given to unlock the resonance field and to be able to access the higher dimensional space has been very important to you. Now that you have begun to sit in this space, we will go into the next component of the work.

What you need to do with these programs is nothing more than a rewiring of the program. You will feel this in a physical way that you have not felt before in energy or healing work. As you begin to work with the catalyst, please dismantle the program through the catalyst. Please also rewire the cellular structure within you that has been holding you in limitation.

So how do we do this? This is going to be the next part of this process.

Dismantling the program itself does not require anything on your behalf. When you are in the higher dimension, it is much easier to work. The only thing that it requires is that you simply offer the program itself to God. That is all you need to do. Yes, you will be working in tandem with God in this process. This is the resonance field that is within you. To summarize, to dismantle the program, you hand over the programs to God that the catalyst has revealed to you. Once you have handed it over from the state of the higher dimension, you can begin to rewire the programs running through you. You can only do this through soul intelligence and Free Will.

Again, your soul intelligence is working with you in this resonance field as you go about this work. You will find information that comes to you as realizations as you are sitting in this space. This information is most likely coming from your soul intelligence. Now, the reason why this information is coming from your soul intelligence is to be able to help you transform the programs within the cellular structure itself. What you will begin to do is not only dismantle these programs, but rewire the cells to be able to hold a whole resonance field, a completely healed and whole resonance field.

What many of you have experienced at times in your life is healing. However, then you quickly revert back to old patterns. This is due to the programs that are running within your cellular structure. So these old programs are what need to change. You have needed to be able to access this state to be able to shift these programs. You will find upon doing this work that this will happen much more quickly and efficiently in the higher dimension than what you have found doing any healing work in the past. Once you access the higher dimension, this work becomes much faster than what it is in the physical dimension.

This is the key piece that has been missing, and this is why your soul intelligence is a crucial integral component in this entire process.

So now, what we need you to do the next time you are sitting in the resonance field is to please go through what you have now identified as your catalyst. Now that you have identified your catalyst, it has been revealed to you what the programs are that are running in your cellular structure. Now that you know the programs that are running through your cellular structure, you can offer these programs over to God. We will begin the process of rewiring the cellular structures so that you can sustain a whole, healed cellular structure without reverting back to the old programs again.

The next time you are sitting in the resonance field, we ask that you simply hand over the programs to God. This is all you need to do right now. We are taking this step by step, day by day, so you can begin to become acclimated to doing this work in the higher dimension.

Please continue to take notes and document your progress.

RECORD 29

YOUR COMMITMENT

What are we going to be discussing today in *Project ONE*? As we get closer to the end of *Project ONE*, you must understand that this is just the first project of what will unfold to become many projects on this topic.

We will return to the interactive portion of this project, the experiential portion of this project. The experiential portion will be the most important section of this entire project because this is the portion in which you are embodying the actual project itself.

As you, the subject matter, move forward in this project, please know that you are a variable. Yes, you are a variable within the project. You are not a *fixed* variable. However, you may be able to change with the project. Therefore, the project can have many outcomes. It can shift in the middle of the project as well, depending upon your commitment to the project and how you do with it. This is not something anybody can control except for you, the subject matter.

So, as you are a variable within the formula of *Project ONE*, we cannot guarantee an outcome. We only present to you the formula for *Project ONE*. As we present the formula to you, you have to understand that this formula is not fixed, but changes along with the variables itself. You, as one of the variables, will have the strongest impact on how the project will shift.

As you embark upon *Project ONE* and do the experiential portion of this work, it is important that you stay committed to it. The reason why it is important that you stay committed to it is because the outcome hinges upon your commitment to participate in the work given to you.

You will not see any outcome if you do this passively. You must be interactively participating in the project. As you stay committed and take accountability, you will begin to see the outcome unfold. The outcome, as we have said before, is the evolved human being as an involved being itself. This is where we are trying to go with *Project ONE*. We are also using this to prove that soul intelligence does exist and can be used to support you in identifying resources that will help your physical landscape move forward. You do not need to know the ins and outs of the multiple dimensions and the higher dimensions in the way that you think you do. Rather, you just need to know how to operate in the higher dimensions.

As a species, you are beginning to access these higher dimensions. And now, what *Project ONE* is doing is showing you how to operate within those dimensions to reveal your infinite potential; and more important, the infinite resources you hold. During the next part, as we go forward in the experiential work of *Project ONE*, you are a variable operating in the higher dimensions. Because of this, you will find yourself in a state that is unfamiliar. Please have awareness as you find yourself in that unfamiliar state in your physical life that this is the work impacting your life.

You will find this state happening rather quickly, and it will be uncomfortable at first. It will be rather uncomfortable at first because what is happening as you participate in the work, as you participate in the project itself, is that you are actually reconfiguring your cellular data. As you reconfigure your cellular data on the higher dimension, this is going to spark a feeling that is new to you, one that you have not experienced in the past because you have become accustomed to the old configuration of the cellular data. This is what has happened. You have believed that the old configuration of the cellular data is who you actually are because this system has been embedded in you for so long. Now, as the system is being dismantled within you, you are experiencing a new feeling or a new you that you have not felt before.

RECORD 30

A COLLECTIVE SOUL

As we move into this next subject, you will still be doing interactive work, but what you have to understand about the work is that this is going to prepare you for what is coming forward. We are preparing you for the future.

Now, what you have to understand is that there will be many projects after this one. There will be a series of projects that will be delivered after this one. You do not get to plan ahead in the project. Rather, each piece will be given to you.

As you do each component of the project, you will be given another component that will be given to you so that you can move forward in the project as necessary. This is to begin to prepare you for what is coming forward in your society as a whole and in your reality as an individual. This is what is coming before you. You do not need to know what the future holds or what it looks like. Rather, you must surrender to it instead. You do not need to know what it looks like. Instead, surrender to what it is. Please surrender to what you are experiencing right now.

Now, what you need to be prepared for as far as what is coming forward for society and for your reality is that your reality is going to change, and it is going to shift as you do this work, but in a way that you are not necessarily expecting. What this means is that you are going to experience an inner realization. As you begin to experience this true inner realization, you will begin to know that everything has happened in the past to prepare you for this coming year. Now, what you have to know about this inner realization is that there is an inner realization happening on the individual level that is also happening on the collective level. As you begin to have this realization of who you truly are and what this means, what this means is that you will begin to experience yourself as you truly are.

As you begin to embark upon this project in the coming year, you will begin to experience yourself as who you truly are. Now, this is going to be frightening and even unnerving at first because you will not understand how you can have this new experience, but what you need to know about this new experience is that it is actually bringing about peace within you. It is bringing inner peace to you. Now what you need to know is that you do not need to fight the inner experience. Rather, you need to embody it. You need to embrace it. As you embrace it, you will experience more peace. If you fight it, you will experience more chaos. You must surrender to it like a wave. If you surrender to it like a wave rather than fighting the wave, you will be embraced by the wave. Rather, if you fight the wave, you will be taken under. That is how this coming year is going to work—much like a wave.

Begin to become comfortable with surrendering to the unknown. As you surrender to the unknown, you will find peace and comfort. Now, what you need to know to be prepared for this upcoming year and this project is that this project is experiential. And yes, we will return to the formula at hand to be able to bring you to the equation and the equalization of being an evolved being. Yes, you will have this as your equalization of being an evolved being—that is where you are going.

This will not happen overnight. Rather, it will happen step by step. But you have to know that what you are seeing in your reality is a great shift. As you see this reality shift, you have to just understand what it is and what is happening. That is all you need to know. So, what you need to do to move forward in this project, to experience what you are experiencing, and what this experience is going to be, again, is to go back and make a commitment to doing this project every day. This is something you need to be committed to doing every day.

What you are doing is accessing an altered dimension. As you access this altered dimension, you will begin to become more comfortable with accessing this dimension. As you begin to access this altered dimension more and more and more, and you become comfortable in the state of this altered dimension, you will begin to work and become interactive in this altered dimension. That is what is happening. You are going to begin to become more interactive in that dimensional space.

And as you become more interactive in that dimensional space, you will become more powerful in being able to impact change in your reality and your society. That is what is happening right here. That is what *Project ONE* is doing. It is bringing you to an altered dimension to be able to impact your physical reality. Yes, this is bridging science and spirituality. It is bridging science and spirituality because as you collect the data, as you begin to collect the data of what is happening as you access this altered dimension, you will be able to understand and prove that soul intelligence does exist.

As soul intelligence is proven valid, you will be able to explain the multidimensional universe, which has begun to be explained by many. And it is known that the multidimensional universe does exist, but it is not proven. It is not proven. That is because you have locked the use of soul intelligence in the past. As you use soul intelligence, you will be able to prove the multidimensional universe.

Soul intelligence has been what has been held in limitation because *you* have been held in limitation. As you break the patterns of limitation from yourself and are able to access soul intelligence, once again you will be able to access the multidimensional universe. Once you are able to access the multidimensional universe, you will be able to do much, much more, and you will be able to understand and prove the existence of the multidimensional universe and soul intelligence.

With respect to soul intelligence, there is individual soul intelligence, but there is also collective soul intelligence. Collective soul intelligence has also been held in limitation just as individual soul intelligence has been held in limitation. So what we are doing in *Project ONE* by doing group and collective work is to help access the collective soul intelligence.

As you access the collective soul intelligence, you can begin to impact your society. Again, you can begin to make actual change in your physical society. As you access the collective soul intelligence, you can begin to make change in that soul intelligence again. It is important that you begin to access collective soul intelligence because when you do so, that collective soul intelligence will help you access that dimension to be able to do work as a collective society in the higher dimensions to make actual change in your collective physical reality. That is what needs to happen. You need to have a collective soul intelligence to be able to come forward, to be able to move forward to do what you need to do.

Now, this collective soul intelligence is the heart of humanity. It is the heart of humanity, and it is the record keeper of humanity. It has kept the data for humanity since the beginning of humanity. So this collective soul intelligence is rather important to the equation.

Collective soul intelligence is seeking to help you and support you in accessing the higher dimensions. It is seeking for you to do this work. However, since it has been held in limitation for so long, what is going to happen as you begin to access collective soul intelligence again is that you will see a dismantling of the attachments that you have been held to as a society. This is similar to what you have gone through as an individual over the past decade, but now you will see it happen more and more at the collective level because the collective soul intelligence is seeking to come through to support you again.

Now, you can only begin to access collective soul intelligence again through collective Free Will. This is very difficult when you say, "Okay, well, if I'm doing the work but the other person isn't, how is this possible?" This is why you will begin to do work as a collective group: because you must learn how to empower each other in your evolution. If you do not empower each other in your evolution, there is no way for you to step forward anymore. This is not possible. You must empower each other in your evolution. If one person has evolved and another person has not, then it is impossible for you to move forward as a collective because the collective soul intelligence is what is going to make an impact in your collective reality. This is how it is going to work.

Therefore, to empower each other as a society is to be able to lift each other and support each other and elevate each other up into the field of God. This means that you do not damn another human being, because as you damn another human being, you will suffer again in the patterns of limitation that you have lived in for so long. So, what needs to happen as you move forward as you support and empower another human being is that you are supporting the collective soul intelligence that is seeking to be expressed. That is what needs to happen as you move forward.

As this collective soul intelligence comes through, this is where your Free Will, again, is required. This is the choice that humanity has right now. This is the choice that humanity has as we embark upon the coming year. This is the choice that humanity has: to be able to empower each other or not. As you make this choice to empower each other, you will be met with love. If you do not choose to empower each other, you will be met with chaos. That is how it will work. So the choice to exert your own Free Will is what you have been given. It is important that you make the choice to choose to love each other and to lift each other up at the cost of yourself, at the cost of your own ego. That is what you have to understand. You may experience some dissatisfaction with yourself. You may experience this, but this is important because this is how you will access collective soul intelligence. This is about humanity moving forward as a collective species. This is not about one human being moving forward as an individual. Because that one human being that moves forward as an individual will not be able to save the human species. It is about the human species moving together as a collective society.

So this is where you are going forward. If there is one human being suffering, if there is one human being in chaos, if there is one human being who has not been able to use their Free Will to choose love, it is your choice. It is simply your choice. It is your Free Will that can then help support them in accessing their own Free Will. This is how it will work. You must use *your* Free Will to support them in accessing *their* own Free Will. This is the only way. This is the only way humanity can move forward as a collective species.

As we begin to go into the next part, we will be doing more interactive work with you. Again, you must stay committed to doing the interactive work every day, to continuing to collect data for this interactive work, and to continuing to understand that you are shifting your cellular data as you are sitting in the space of the feminine resonance, as you are sitting in that energetic field. Remember, this is an energetic field that lives through you and around you.

So you will begin to sit in the space in the feminine resonance field, and as you access the feminine resonance field and as you sit in the space of the feminine resonance field, this will be a huge undertaking to be able to heal this energetic field, but you will be doing so with God, as you call it. And what will happen is that you and your soul intelligence and your Free Will and God will be able to access the feminine resonance field so that you can sustain a healed feminine resonance field, and you will begin to alter the cellular data that exists within you. As you begin to alter the cellular data that exists within you, you will begin to see a shift in your reality.

RECORD 31

A NEW HUMAN

What we are going to be discussing today in this new process that you are all embarking upon, this new kind of work you are all embarking upon, is a new kind of work. Yes, it is a new kind of work. And the reason why it is a new kind of work is because this work requires not only your participation but your choice as well. This work requires your choice. It requires you to make a higher choice *now*.

As we move forward, as we prepare you for what is coming in the new world, as we prepare you for what is coming in your new humanity, your new humanity is very good. Yes, it is. Indeed, it is. What you need to know about this new humanity is that you have abilities that are far superior to what you have ever realized before in history. There have been ancient civilizations and many civilizations that have had abilities, but the abilities now are being progressed. They are being progressed. As humanity progresses, *your* abilities progress, and this is what is happening.

Now, this is not about your abilities as much as it is about your alignment to God and what your alignment to God truly is; it is your alignment to your truest highest form of yourself. That is what your alignment is, to your truest highest form of yourself. Now, this is not dismissing God. No, it is not dismissing God. But this is for you to understand that what is within you and what you are made of is the highest form of God. And what you have to know as we move forward into *Project ONE* is that the actual physics of what you are doing in this process and moving dimensionally and working with other human beings is quite enduring.

The reason why it is enduring is because it will take great sustainability for you to be able to work in the other dimensions.

Regarding the physics of this exercise, this is a complicated lesson, and it will take much more than *Project ONE* to be able to explain this to you, but we want you to begin to understand the foundational explanation of the physics of what you are doing. As we expand the teaching, as we move and progress into the teaching, you will understand more. Right now, we are introducing *Project ONE* to you. We are introducing you to the foundation of working in a different dimension, the foundation of making an impact in your physical reality from a different dimension and the possibility of you being able to change your cellular structure yourself with the help of God. You cannot do this alone. This is the contract. Indeed, it is.

So why are you working with other people? Why are you working with your partner and within groups? You will need to support each other in this process, and this will help you dissipate the boundaries that you have created between one another. So, this is an important component within the equation of *Project ONE*. Now, what you have to understand about the actual physics of moving interdimensionally is that this is very important. And the reason why is because we are talking about energy here. We are talking about energy, the energy that lives within the physical dimension. This is what you are working with when you are shifting dimensions. You all have the ability to do this quite easily.

You have the physical body that lives within the physical dimension, but there is a component within you that lives in all dimensions. That is your soul intelligence. Yes, it is. It is your soul that can access all dimensions, but you are working specifically with your soul intelligence that can access all dimensions here and now.

So what is your soul intelligence doing within you? What you have to understand is that your soul intelligence consists of energy. It consists of energy, and that is the energetic resonance system. Now, why you are going to have a complicated time understanding this is because you have not really begun to understand energy and the scope in which it needs to be understood.

Energy is a generic word. What we are talking about today is the energetic system, and what you were conceived of during creation. Your soul was actually conceived from an energetic system, and this is how this teaching will continue—to be able to explain how your soul was actually conceived. That is the evolution of *Project ONE*—to explain to you how your soul was actually conceived energetically within the universe, within the actual energy system of the universe.

Now, this is not just about energy. This is about how you integrate and how you operate from these different dimensions and how you begin to work in these different dimensions to impact your reality. This is also about your resonance systems—all your different resonance systems within you and the different resonances that you have within you. We started this project by talking about the feminine resonance system and the importance of the feminine resonance system within the female body and the male body. What you need to know about the resonance system within the female body and the male body is something you have been working with daily since you have begun this project.

What you will begin to experience as you do this is a shift in your physical reality. Now, this shift in your physical reality means that there is going to be a shift in your physical mind and your physical operation—meaning that you are going to be operating from a different state of being. The reason why is because you are actually changing the programs within the feminine resonance system. What you have to know about this is that all the cellular data that you carry is unique. It is unique to you. All the cellular data that is within each of your cells is unique to you.

Now, this energetic system has data running through it. Know that not all data is the same; rather, data is different within you so you hold various patterns of data within you and within the different resonances. This is very confusing. All you need to know is that the feminine resonance system holds its own unique pattern within it. It holds its own unique programs within it so you are working right now to make those programs whole again so that they are no longer distorted. Right now, you are simply working with that. That is all you are working with right now.

As we move forward from *Project ONE* into the evolution of *Project ONE*, you will see how different resonance systems work. But for right now, you are just working with the feminine resonance system. So, where we left off was you beginning to work with your partners, working with your partners accessing the higher dimensions and beginning to do work on your actual programs, your catalyst in your programs to be able to make those whole again with God. That is where we left off.

Now, you will begin to see these actual programs transform as you do this every day. What we have to explain to you is that Free Will never goes away. Free Will never goes away, so you have to continue to do this. You have to continue to do this work in order for the programs to have a long-lasting impact. This is very important to the outcome. This will be very important to the outcome of *Project ONE*.

All you need to know about today, all you need to know to move forward, is something about you, yourself. It is important that you stay committed to the work, but what else do you need to know, you ask.

As you begin speaking, the energy will move through you. The energy will speak. The energy will move through you in a way that it needs to move through you. But this can only happen once you begin speaking what you need to know as you move forward. And then, you embark upon this path. As we move into this next stage, this next stage of *Project ONE*, and what this next stage will be, will be very important because this is the stage where you will be bringing *Project ONE* to more people.

Now, you have thought that you have made this information public. You have *not* made the information public yet. In the coming month, you will begin to make this information more public. As we have said, in the following two months, all of the information will become much more public.

What you have to understand is that you must stay humble in this process. But also, the work will unfold as it needs to unfold. You do not need to do anything but stay committed to the actual process of doing the meditation and doing the channeling. This is all you need to do. You do not need to make plans, as the plans have already been predetermined in many ways. All you need to do is use your Free Will to simply choose this energy every day.

As you choose this energy and you choose to embody this energy, you become an emissary of the energy, and that is happening now. As you become a sample, as you become a subject for the work, a subject matter for the whole earth, you can use it to prove to other people why you are using your Free Will to stay committed to the work at hand. You must stay committed to the work at hand because you are the subject matter.

This is very important for you to know, and especially as you embark upon the next few months, as this work becomes more publicly known and as the transcription is made available to other people. This will be happening soon. This will be happening in 2020. The work will accelerate quickly as long as you use your Free Will to stay committed to the actual energetic practice of the work and are able to become the subject matter for the work itself. This is the most important component, and this is something you need to understand as a channel. You are not *just* a channel. You are the subject matter as well. So, your participation is needed in order to make the project valid. You are proving validity for this actual project itself. Therefore, you need to stay committed to the energetic process of the work.

Now, there will be much going on. This is why it is important to move at a quick and accelerated pace, as we want this to move efficiently and seamlessly. As long as you do not resist with your own fear-based projections, this will be able to move efficiently and seamlessly. This is all you need to do. You need to stay committed to your practice, to take advantage of this work. You will be able to move forward much easier than if you have any kind of resistance. Please understand that you must do this work every single day in order for it to move forward in the way that we would like it to move forward.

RECORD 32

THE TUNNEL OF LIFE EXPLAINED

Now, where we left off discussing the higher human is what you need to understand about the actual awakening of God within us. There is nothing you need to do for that process to happen. What you need to be concerned about right now is simply accessing your Free Will to choose your soul intelligence and to go about the protocol that we have given you in *Project ONE* so far. Once you become accustomed to this protocol, you will become more acclimated to working in the higher dimension. Once you are more acclimated to working in a new dimensional space, there will be more work that you can do to impact your physical reality. Right now, all we want you to do is acclimate to working with the feminine resonance field.

Project ONE and the protocol that we are giving you here is taking you step by step to evolving into a higher human. However, there will be more beyond this book. There will be a significant amount more beyond this, but what you have to do now as a species is to prevent yourself from experiencing any kind of cataclysm. To do so as a species, you must access your Free Will to call your soul intelligence into being, and to be able to do this as often as possible—preferably, daily.

As you go through this process during the day, you will begin to see a rapid shift. This is the foundational work of this project. In order to move efficiently, you have to be able to understand the foundation of this project. This project will have layers to it. However, first you need to become grounded and solid in the foundation. As you become grounded in the foundation of this project, you will begin to immediately experience a difference, and impact your reality as your individual self and as a group.

This project will be delivered rather quickly. The layers upon this project will be delivered quickly as well. However, please take the time to understand and acclimate to the feminine resonance. The reason why the feminine resonance is so important is because of the female body and the distortion within the female and healing her to her rightful place. At this point, we can circle back to the beginning, where we explained to you that the feminine resonance lives within the womb of the female body. The feminine resonance lives within the womb in the female body, and it lives within the heart of the male body.

This feminine resonance field lives within the physical body, but it also lives within the multidimensional universe. What you are doing in this work is accessing the multidimensional universe, and it is being reflected back into the physical body. You are making actual shifts within the physical body itself and within the cells that this physical body holds, so you are making an actual impact into the female womb and into the male heart. This is how you are incarnating as a species.

It is crucial that the feminine resonance field is made whole again. As you incarnate as a human species, you are coming through the multidimensional universe in order to incarnate into the physical plane. There is a process you go through when you incarnate from the multidimensional universe into the physical plane. It is the process of transferring through a tunnel. This is not the tunnel that you all thought it was going to be, but rather, it is a tubelike tunnel that exists on an energetic grid.

This is an energetic grid that is meant to bridge the multidimensional universe with the physical plane. This tunnel that bridges both dimensions exists within the female body on the physical plane. These are the tubes within the female womb. These tubes are represented in the multidimensional universe as an energetic grid that brings the life from the higher dimension into the physical plane or into the physical womb. When souls are incarnated into this physical womb, they go from a higher energetic grid into a dense energetic grid, and this is a painful process. This is what many of you are beginning to realize as you discuss various birth methods. Many of you are beginning to realize that birth can be traumatic, because it is a painful process.

There is nothing that you can do to alter this. The cause is the shift from the higher energies into the denser energy of the physical plane. However, during this time on the planet, the dense energy is changing to be able to vibrate at a faster speed so that you can access those higher energies easier. The physical dimension is changing and shifting itself, and you are acclimating within that physical dimension. The reason why we have begun *Project ONE* with the feminine resonance field is because once we can make the feminine resonance field whole again, the energetic grid of the female womb will shift. Once that has shifted to vibrate at a higher accelerated speed, the birthing process will not be as painful, and therefore, when you do not have any trauma in the birthing process, you are born without trauma. That is what we are going through.

We are giving you an ability to birth a higher human being. As you are able to birth a higher human being, you will begin to raise a planet of higher human beings.

This all begins in the actual birthing process. It begins with conceiving the soul into the female womb. It is not until the female womb has been made whole that the birthing process can be liberated. When we say the birthing process, we mean the process of conceiving the soul into the womb, not the birth of the physical being into the physical world, but rather the birth of the soul into the womb. The soul has already been conceived. The soul is conceived with creation. Once the soul is born into the womb, into the physical being, this is where the birth actually happens. It does not happen when the child is born into the world. It happens when the soul is born into the world. The soul is born into the world before the child is born into the world. The soul is born into the world with conception.

Now, what you have to understand about making this feminine resonance field whole is that it is something vastly important in the male body as well. This lives within the heart center. This is the part of conception that is important for the male as well, which comes from the male heart. It is felt through the process of love from the male heart. This is not to dismiss the fact that it does not happen through the female's heart as well. But the male's heart has a certain energetic grid to it in the process of conception when it comes to pulling the soul into the female body that opens up an energetic vessel. It opens up a gateway for the soul to be able to come into this physical plane, depending on the heart space of the man.

RECORD 33
THE TRANSMISSION

What will we be discussing today? What you have to know about where we are moving forward in this first month of the new year is that this information that is being transcribed will be here for a long time. What you must know about the information being transmitted is that it is being transmitted with a higher integrity to it. The channel is able to transmit this information due to the work that she has done herself. This is important to the transmission of this information.

You, the reader, will be able to receive this information in a way that would not be able to be so due to the transmitter doing the work already. The transmission of the work is important to the outcome of *Project ONE*. There is a code to this project. We have said before that this is a multidimensional project.

The code to this project is energetic. As you are experiencing the work, you are feeling the work as well. This is made possible through the actual transmission of the work. It has taken the transmission of the work to be energetically coded to make this possible.

Now, what you also have to understand about this work is that as you become more interactive in the work itself, as you become more participatory, the work will become multidimensional and more layered. It will become increasingly multidimensional and multilayered as you become more interactive in it.

Now, you ask what the actual space that you are accessing is. You are accessing the feminine resonance energetic field. That is what you are accessing. This is an actual energetic field in a different dimension. Now, what you have to understand about the parallel universes or the parallel dimensions is that when you are accessing a different dimension, there are many various dimensions that you can access. There is not just one parallel universe or infinite parallel universes. The particular universe that you are accessing, the particular dimension that you are accessing, is a dimension where humanity has always been able to access to be able to do this work.

This particular dimension that you are working in, this particular field that you are working in, was created for this reason. It was created for you to be able to access your own soul intelligence and your own powers within. That is what this dimensional space was created for.

Now, what you have to understand about this dimensional space and what makes it different from the physical space that you live in is that this dimensional space is accessed through consciousness alone. When you move into any other dimension, you do not have the physical body; you only have your soul intelligence or your soul. This exists here and now, always, so just because you live in the physical plane does not mean you cannot access those other dimensions. You can access those other dimensions anytime you wish, whether in this life or after this life—or in any other life. This is all possible because within you, you have the component that makes you a multidimensional human being.

The physical body lives within the physical dimension. It is a container for you in the physical dimension to be able to experience the physical dimension for what it is, which is nothing more than a mirror. It is a reality. It is a reality that you have created as a mirror for you to be able to see your own consciousness. You work through this physical world for the actual expansion of your consciousness. So, while your physical body is a container for your consciousness, it feels restraint. Your consciousness feels restrained from the physical body. Your consciousness is much more expansive than the physical body that you hold. Your consciousness is always and will always be much more expansive than the physical body you hold. Therefore, because your consciousness is physically expansive, you are able to access those multidimensions anytime you like.

Once you begin doing this work in the multidimensional fields and in the multidimensional universe, you will find that you can do a lot of work to impact your physical reality within the multidimensional spaces. Regarding the physical field or the physical landscape that you live in, that your body lives in, it is important that you take good care of your body. Your body is holding your consciousness itself. While your consciousness is more expansive than your body, your body is also holding your consciousness.

Your physical body acts as a container for your experience in the physical landscape. Your physical body is nothing more than a container for the physical landscape. It can reflect back to you your consciousness as well. So when you look at your physical body, when you feel your physical body, you can know that this is a reflection of your consciousness because it is a container for your consciousness.

If your consciousness itself is holding certain energetic strings in it, and it is holding a certain energy system, know that this can impact your physical body just as the multidimensional universe can impact the physical universe. However, the physical universe cannot impact the multidimensional universe. This is how it works. Therefore, your physical body cannot impact your consciousness. While you may think it can, it actually cannot. It is your consciousness that impacts your physical body. That is how it works.

When you look at your physical body, know that your physical body is a representation of what is happening in the consciousness, what is happening in the multidimensional space. As you begin to do this work, you will begin to see a shift, and you will begin to see a change in your physical reality and in your physical body. And as you begin to see that shift and change in your physical reality and physical body, it will be a confirmation to you that you have begun to do the work of *Project ONE*. This is what this means.

PART FOUR

THE COLLECTIVE MISSION

RECORD 34

HEALING

What will we be discussing today in *Project ONE*? As we move forward as a collective species, what will be happening as this work begins to integrate more and you begin to move forward as a collective species is that you will begin to dissipate the boundaries between you. As boundaries become dissipated, it will become increasingly easier to do the consciousness work. It works in parallel at an accelerated pace.

As you embark upon this work, you have the hardest task in front of you because the boundaries are so dense. As the boundaries dissipate and become thinner between humanity, between each person, between each concept, each idea, each thought that you believe yourself to be, these boundaries begin to dissipate. As they dissipate, the consciousness work and the healing work become much easier.

So what this work will seek to do is begin with a group where this will take place. It will take place within a container itself. So as you become a part of this group, as you begin to do this work, the boundaries will begin to dissipate within the group. As the boundaries begin to dissipate within the group, the work becomes easier within the group. This is the container. This is the test container in which we will sample *Project ONE* to begin to see how rapidly you are able to heal yourselves in your environment, your reality as you know it to be. This is what will be happening.

As you begin to do this work as a group, your commitment will be rather important to the outcome of *Project ONE*. As we circle back to the formula of *Project ONE*, we have begun to identify the various variables within *Project ONE*. As we have identified the variables within *Project ONE*, we will lay out the entire formula.

You are not fully prepared for this yet; rather, you are *being* prepared. You're being prepared as you become participatory in the work itself. Where we are leaving you is in the space of the feminine resonant field. We want to leave you understanding the feminine resonance field quite well and being comfortable working within the field.

We would like you to return back to the feminine resonance field today, back to that energetic field. You can now become more interactive in that field by doing work on each other, not just yourself. You now understand this concept of reprogramming your own cellular data. And this is very possible to do. You understand that you use the code of 333 to begin to access the data within the feminine resonance field itself. This is what has brought you to this place.

Now, you can begin to work on each other as well. It is important to grow and evolve as a collective group because as you evolve as a collective group and you begin to work on each other, this is going to support the dissipation of boundaries itself. What we want to do next as you begin to access this energetic field is to have you begin to work on each other. Now you ask, "Is this crossing boundaries with another person?" No. If somebody is giving consent, if one person has given consent to the other to begin to work on them, then they choose it of their own Free Will. If you cannot heal each other, then how do you ever heal?

You ask, "Can energies between two people become intertwined or exchanged?" What you have to know about doing energy work on each other is that you are doing this work in a protective container. It is the dimensional space that you are working on that will support you in this process. There is nothing that will harm you as far as doing work on each other from this dimensional space. Your intention in doing this work is your greatest asset and will give you protection in this space. Therefore, when you do this work, you must hold a clear intention that you are doing this for the highest good of humanity and for the collective evolution of humanity. This is a requirement.

Now, as we go back to being in the space, being in the higher dimension, and as you begin to do work on each other and you have set this as an intention, to be working for the highest good of humanity, then you can begin to do this work knowing that nothing will harm you. You can have faith in that.

As you begin to do this work on each other, you must hold and support each other in this energetic space. As you hold and support each other in this energetic space, you are not only dissipating boundaries, you are healing. You are doing healing work on another human being. This is the potential that every single human being has within them, to be a healer. Every human being has this capacity. It is a matter of accessing the space to do it. That is all that it is. What we are doing now is empowering you to do actual work on one another.

Now, as you begin to do this work, and you begin to document, to take notes of what you are experiencing, you will be able to collect data as a group. The importance of this will be monumental to the outcome of *Project ONE*. It is the actual data that you will be collecting where you will find your own and each other's progression.

In addition, the cellular DNA will begin to change within you. So, many of you will experience a physical shift as you do this work. This physical shift is nothing more than the physical landscape changing and shifting, as we have said before. Now, as this physical landscape shifts within your physical body, it will also shift in your physical reality as well. And this is okay. The most important aspect of this that you must know is to not resist this shift or to not resist this change, but rather, embrace it. This will be important as well to the outcome of your own healing within *Project ONE*.

Now, also, as you begin to access this space in the feminine resonance and energetic field and you begin to do work on each other, what this actually means is that you actually set the intention for another human being for their highest good and for their program.

RECORD 35

THE FOUNDATION

What will we be discussing today in *Project ONE*? What you have to know as we move forward, as we begin to end the first foundation, is that this is the first foundation of *Project ONE*. This is what this will be titled, *Project ONE, Foundation ONE*.

What you have to understand about *Project ONE, Foundation ONE* is that this is the foundation. Therefore, it is important that the foundation be built correctly. What we mean by this is if you build a house and the foundation of the house is not built correctly, then the house will fall down over time. This is the reason why *Foundation ONE* is crucial to the development of *Project ONE*.

Please know that *Project ONE, Foundation ONE* is an introduction. This is an introduction for you to begin to interact with the multidimensional aspect of you.

As you begin to participate in the multidimensional aspects of yourself, you will begin to do much, much more. But what we want you to do is simply begin to participate in the multidimensional aspects of yourself. This will be an important foundation for you, so please do it as much as you possibly can.

Now we will return to codes and how these codes work with your cellular data more as we go further into *Project ONE*. Now, what we also want to leave you with in *Foundation ONE* is to have an understanding of how you can begin to implement *Project ONE* into your daily life now, and how it can impact your daily life.

Many of you are seeking relief from your daily life in the immediate term. Many of you desire healing, a more peaceful life, clarity, and happiness. It is possible to impact your physical reality simply by committing to the practices given to you in *Project ONE*. This is all you need to do.

Now, how you impact your physical reality is what you want to know—how you have the programs within you that you identified as manifesting your physical reality. The programs that you have taken time to identify in your life are driving the manifestation of your entire physical reality. Now, as these programs are shifted through *Project ONE*, you will begin to manifest a new reality in alignment with your higher power, or God. This is how this project will unfold.

As we have said before, this is bridging science and spirituality. It is bridging science and spirituality by employing your soul intelligence, and soul intelligence is the bridge. Scientists have gone so far working from the limited mind. The key component that they are missing is soul intelligence. Once soul intelligence is put to work, as it is waiting to be, you will be able to bridge science and spirituality, because every single human being will be able to fulfill the potential that is required to move forward as a species.

Now, what you also have to understand as you move forward with *Project ONE* and are beginning to utilize your soul intelligence is that your soul intelligence has tremendous knowledge within it because it is the record keeper of your history, or the history of your soul. Therefore, the knowledge that will be coming to you during this time will be tremendous. You will experience revelations during this time. Recognize it as your soul intelligence, and you do not need to question it. If you begin to question and hesitate, this is where the work will become tricky. Do not question and hesitate. You know the truth. When it is first presented to you or expressed in consciousness, you will recognize it as truth. This is your soul intelligence. Please have trust in that, and do not question it.

As you allow yourself to have trust in your soul intelligence again, it will begin to guide you where you need to go. This will unfold in your life naturally. You do not need to consciously manifest anything. All you need to do is simply allow yourself to surrender this work to your higher power within the higher dimensional space.

This foundation is giving you the keys to accessing the higher dimensional space. That is what the foundation is. The foundation is also having you begin to work as a collective group.

As we continue with *Project ONE* in the near future, we will begin to uncover more for you in terms of working with various codes and cellular data. This will greatly impact the trajectory of humanity and the concept of healing work. Working with codes in the multidimensional space to heal programs within your cellular data is the beginning. You have just begun to do this in *Project ONE* with the feminine resonance and its code of 333.

This has just been the beginning. However, you could say it is the most critical part because it is the foundation. As the feminine resonance and you come into balance on the physical plane, you will see the massive impact in your reality. Please remember that the feminine resonance field is perfect in the multidimensional universe. It is only in the physical plane that it is distorted. As you bring it into balance by recognizing its perfection, by accessing and embodying it from the multidimensional space, you will be able to heal the feminine resonance field.

Once you are able to do this, the impact that you will see in your reality will shift, but you will also see the programs that are running through you as healing. Please access this space as much as possible, because as you access that space, you begin to embody it and ground it into the physical dimension.

As you work together as a collective group, you are there to support each other and help each other in this process. You cannot do it alone. Humanity can learn this either consequentially or preemptively through its own Free Will. You can choose to know that you need each other to move forward or you can learn through consequences. It will be much smoother to choose this of your own Free Will.

Once you learn to support and help each other in this process that you are evolving from, that you are growing from, it will become easier because your energetic levels, your energetic system that is composed of higher energies, will become stronger as you do this simply because you are giving to one another. That is how the higher energies live—through the process of giving.

As you give, you will receive. This is an old saying, but it is true of the energetic system within you. As you give, those higher energies will become more magnified. They will be nourished. And that is all you are doing: nourishing those energies. So what we want to say about *Project ONE* is to please use the protocol that has been given as much as possible.

RECORD 36
COLLECTIVE EVOLUTION

What we want to discuss today in *Project ONE* as we are nearing the end of the foundational material is one last interactive project for you to begin to practice and implement.

You have now acclimated yourself to sitting in the multidimensional space. From here you will become more participatory. We want to leave you with one last exercise within the foundational material.

You know the protocol already, as you have been taught to be able to access the feminine resonance field. You have made the intention that you are doing this for the highest good of humanity while also healing the programs that are currently running through your system.

The last component of the interactive process is to dissipate the boundaries between you and your partner or group, whichever you are working with now. We have discussed the importance of dissipating boundaries between you and your partner or you and the group that you are working with, but please know that the boundaries being dissipated happen as a result of the energy itself.

Now, you have already begun to work in groups or in partners when you are doing this exercise. Again, if you do not have a group or partner that you feel comfortable doing this with, the partner will be revealed to you within your life. This is how this work will occur. You have to trust this process as you do it with yourself every day. As you access this space and sit within this space in your group or with your partner, you have begun to identify and heal the programs within your cellular data.

To dissipate these boundaries is to *merge* with your group or with your partner. You are *merging* the collective field. This process will continue into the next level of *Project ONE*. However, we would like you to experience this idea of *merging* and to implement it now so that you can see where you will be going between now and the next level of *Project ONE*—between the foundational level and the next level. This collective work as you begin to merge boundaries will support you in individual healing as well.

And the way this works, the way it will support you in your individual healing in the individual healing of the programs in your cellular data, is that you will be merging energetic fields with another human being. Now this sounds scary at first because you have become frightened of this concept of merging energetic fields with another person; however, in the multidimensional landscape, your energetic fields are already merged. You have an oversoul where these energetic systems are already merged.

So what you are doing in the physical landscape and the process of merging your energetic systems to dissipate the form between you and another is this: when you begin to access this space, the feminine resonance field, and you are sitting with your partner or group, all you need to do—with the use and support of your soul intelligence and God—is to make the intention to dissipate the forms between you both.

As you make that intention, the work will be done. That is all you need to do to make the intention to dissipate the forms between you in love with the support of your soul intelligence and God. As you begin to do this, you will notice that the forms between you actually begin to dissipate. You know yourself in a state of *ONE*. You will begin to understand this concept more as you move forward in *Project ONE*. However, we want to leave you with this one last interactive component, this one last interactive exercise, within *Foundation ONE*.

Now, you have to understand that *Foundation ONE*, the interactive work that you have done so far, has been complicated. However, it has also been seamless. The reason we say it has been complicated is because the physics of what you are doing is beyond what you have known yourself to be capable of in the past. However, with the use of your soul intelligence, it has become possible. It has become a possibility within the physical landscape and within the multidimensional landscape.

As you move forward in the interactive component of *Project ONE,* we ask if you could please keep notes about what is happening. You need to keep notes and record what is happening within your physical life and within your physical landscape as you do this work. This will support you in being able to understand where you began and where you have progressed.

As an entity, you will work together. When you collect this data, it will be living proof of *Project ONE* in your physical reality because it will show you where you begin and where you have progressed. As each person collects the data and the data is tallied, you will see a significant theme running through it. That significant theme will become the living component of the formula. You will become the living component of the formula that we will continue to lay out as we move forward with *Project ONE* in additional levels.

Now you ask, "What if while doing this work, a problem comes to surface or a problem begins to arise? What if something begins to arise that I'm uncomfortable with?"

You do not need to pay it too much attention. Please continue to do this work and access the space. As you do this, the conflict or the inner tension that you are experiencing will dissipate and be realigned as your cellular data is being realigned to the truth of who you are. This is the realignment to the Truth of you operating as God in Action. That is what is happening right now.

This is a realignment. During any realignment, the old is brought forth to be relinquished. To relinquish, please continue to do the work that has been outlined here. That is all you need to do. When something comes up that is uncomfortable, please do not look at it too much. Just know that it has been there, and now it is fleeting. As long as you sustain working in this dimensional space, the higher energy will do the work for you.

It is God working in tandem with your soul intelligence, using your Free Will to make this so. This allows the energy of the multidimensional space to do the heavy lifting. You can say that you are doing the work, but please know that it is not your ego doing the work. It is your soul intelligence and God doing the work. Your work is making the choice for it to be so.

RECORD 37
YOUR UNIQUE SYSTEM

As we begin the last section of *Project ONE*, you must begin to know "of yourself" in this new way. Now, what does this mean, to know of yourself in this new way? It means "of yourself" as a multidimensional human being. That is what it means. It means that you are no longer a human being in the physical dimension only. It means that you are a human being accessing all dimensions. That is what it means. This is the new human being—the human being who can access all dimensions at any given point in time.

Now, as you know of yourself in this new way, as you know of yourself as a human being who can access these dimensions in a way that you have not been able to before, you can understand yourself as having a greater power within. What you have to understand about this power is how it is being used. That is very important to the outcome of *Project ONE*: how you can begin to use this power and what the intention is in being able to use this power.

Now, as we have explained throughout the foundation of *Project ONE*, this is physics. This resonance system that we are introducing to you is nothing more than physics. The bridging of science and spirituality is nothing more than accessing soul intelligence.

As you embark upon *Project ONE*, the intention with which you do this is going to impact your work. You will not see a benefit if it is not being used correctly. This must be used in alignment with your Free Will to choose love in all aspects of your life.

Please begin to activate your Free Will to choose love in all aspects of your life, in every aspect of your life. As you choose God and you choose love, you will be able to access soul intelligence effortlessly. When you access soul intelligence effortlessly, you will be able to go about this experiment effortlessly as well. It will be seamless because the cells that you are made of will be vibrating at a higher rate. Your cells will be vibrating at a higher speed. And when that happens, that means that the density that you hold will be less. When the density that you hold is less, that means you have less form. This does not mean that you actually lose your physical body. It means that your physical body begins vibrating at a higher speed. When it vibrates at a higher speed, when the cellular structure vibrates at a faster speed, you can access these dimensions faster. You can access your soul intelligence seamlessly. This only happens through Free Will and consciously choosing love and God.

We have mentioned before that claiming Free Will is the prerequisite to *Project ONE*. This will be an important component throughout the entire project because if you do not begin the project correctly, you will have distorted outcomes.

As we mentioned before, you are a perfect human being. Because you are a perfect human being, you can know that everything inside you is perfect as it is. When we say that your cellular structure is distorted, when we say that the resonance within you is distorted, we mean only on the physical dimension. In all other dimensions, you are perfect. You are perfect. What you are doing when you are accessing these other dimensions is accessing yourself as a perfect, whole human being. You are embodying that human being into the physical dimension. You are integrating that being into the physical dimension. As you integrate that being into the physical dimension, it begins to heal the physical body—all aspects of the physical body.

As you move forward into the participatory work, the interactive work, the shift is happening. The cellular-structure shift is occurring within you. Please know that the programs that are being shifted represent the DNA within you. It is the DNA that you are reprogramming. The DNA that is in the physical dimension, the physical body, *is* the resonance system in the higher dimensions.

To understand the DNA and the resonance system, know that the DNA is representative of the resonance system in the physical dimension. This is why when we say that every human being has a unique resonance system, every human being has a unique set of DNA. This is what you are reprogramming. Please know that you *did* choose the DNA that lives inside you. This is what you are made of. This DNA is not new to you in this lifetime. The DNA has been with you for all lifetimes, and it is always evolving. This is not something that is only of the physical dimension. This is of *all* dimensions. It exists in all dimensions as the resonance system.

Similar to DNA, each human being has a unique resonance system. While you are all the same made in the image of God, you are also all unique. The resonance system derives from one resonance, and this one resonance lives within every human being, just as there is a DNA strand that lives within every human being.

So, while you have DNA, you all have a unique code to your DNA programs; you have one component of your DNA that is all the same, and this is what makes you human. This is what makes you a human being. However, what you have to know is that because your DNA is unique, your resonance system is also unique. Now, what this means is that how you were conceived as a soul, the resonance system that you came into being with, that your soul came into being with, is unique. Your soul came into being with a unique resonance system.

Now, let us return to where we left you last in the participatory work—working in groups or partners to dissipate the boundaries that you have created. These are boundaries of form that you have created in the physical space. However, what we want to discuss with you is that not only are you the same and these boundaries can be dissipated, but you are also each unique. You are unique, and this gives you your own set of circumstances in this lifetime to learn through. So, not one of you will learn through the same circumstances. You must know this to support each other in your healing. So, while you are moving toward a collective transition, a collective healing, you are also coming into this life with a unique set of circumstances that you are all learning through. You must respect that within each other.

So, while your boundaries are dissipating, you are each learning through a unique process as well. Therefore, you cannot project your own process to somebody else, or place expectations on another. You will never understand what the person beside you is learning. You may be empathetic, you may be compassionate and sensitive, and you may be able to support them, but to truly support somebody in their own learning and in their own growth is to be able to respect them. You must respect them and their own process because they have a unique resonance system, a unique DNA that is giving them their own set of circumstances to learn through in this lifetime. Therefore, you can never hold anybody accountable to the same experience that you are holding yourself accountable to.

As you move forward in the group work, in the participatory work that you will be doing together, you must respect each other in their own lessons. Not only must you respect the person that you are working with on this project, but you must also respect every person that you encounter during this time. If you wish to evolve as a collective species, you must respect every human being that you encounter during this time. This is very important to the outcome of *Project ONE*, and it is even more important to your collective growth.

This will support the boundaries in dissipating because you are beginning to respect and understand each other as unique human beings with unique systems. You all have a unique DNA program that you are reprogramming. As you reprogram your system, be in alignment with truth, be in alignment with God. That is what is happening. We ask that you continue this work every day, that you do this work *every single day.*

RECORD 38

ONE

In the foundational material of *Project ONE*, we have introduced you to many components, including your ability to work in a multidimensional space, as well as your ability to access yourselves as a collective species. As a collective species, the code of one is the code of the higher human. This is the code of the higher human. This is the code of the higher human because the higher human comes without the form of the physical dimension. The physical dimension can evolve into a space where you can exist without the form you know yourself to be in now.

Now, this does not make sense at first. You ask, "How can we evolve without our form?" You can continue to evolve, and that is the purpose of the physical dimension. It is for your evolution. However, the higher human, which is coded by the number one, is the code of the higher human of the collective human without the density of form. You will always be evolving in the physical dimension, and that is why the physical dimension was created.

We are not taking away the physical dimension. All we are doing is making you aware of your ability to access an alternate dimension in which you can work from and know yourselves without the dense form that you know yourselves in today. This will be done, as we have just mentioned, through the collective work.

The code of *ONE* is relevant to *Project ONE* because humanity is moving into a collective species represented by the number *one*. Hence, that is the reason this material is called *Project ONE*

Many of you are beginning to awaken to this, to your oneness. This is a conversation that has been happening for years. The new piece that is being introduced in *Project ONE*, which is the project toward your oneness, toward your collective humanity, the project that we will be explaining to you as far as how to embark into your oneness as one species, is only done through this collective work. It is done through this collective work.

Through this collective work, you will need to witness each other in a new light in order to make this possible. That is witnessing the God within each other. As you begin sitting in your groups or with your partner to do the work of *Project ONE*—the project that is bringing you into your oneness—you will be required to see God within each other. Now, this is not a new concept to you. However, to put it into action is more than occasionally seeing the God within each other at your discretion. It will require the use of your Free Will to make the choice to love each other unconditionally, even in the face of adversity, pain, or hurt. This you will need to practice with every human being that you encounter throughout your day, week, month, or year. This is critical to the healing—to the healing of the planet and to the healing of the species.

This is the project toward your oneness—these foundational concepts of practicing collective spiritual work to propel you toward your oneness as a species, and also the foundational concepts of bridging science and spirituality through your use of soul intelligence, which you only choose through Free Will. These foundational concepts, these two concepts, are extremely important to *Project ONE*. We want you to understand that these foundational concepts must be used by you in order to move forward.

Now, we must also explain the foundational concept of the multidimensional space and being able to work in that space, and also your collective oneness and how you will move toward collective oneness. The third concept that we have explained is the resonance system—the resonance system as a whole, in its entirety.

We have touched upon the feminine resonance system in the foundational concepts, but as *Project ONE* unfolds more and as we bring more work forth, you can begin to see the formula that will be outlined in all of *Project ONE*. The resonances we have just begun to touch upon but the resonance system within humanity and all of creation is going to be very important and will be explained in much more depth. But returning to *Project ONE*, what you can also understand about your oneness and about what it is to be *ONE* is that the resonance system that we have begun to introduce in *Project ONE* that you need to understand is that creation began with one resonance. It began with one resonance. This one resonance then split off into many resonances. It split off first into three resonances, and then many resonances split off from there.

All of these resonances represent different energetic codes that work within each human being. However, because all of these resonances were created from one resonance, that one resonance exists within every single human being. You will be returning again to that one resonance of creation. So, while you each have a unique energetic system from the split of these resonances, which will be explained in much more detail as *Project ONE* goes forward, there is one resonance that also exists within you. So, you have many codes to these resonance systems, but there is one resonance or one DNA that exists within all of humanity, and this is what makes you one.

RECORD 39
THE BEGINNING

We meet today with what is a congratulations for coming to this place within *Project ONE*. This is a congratulations. We are congratulating you for being able to evolve as a species to a place where you can do this work collectively. We are also congratulating you because this is just the beginning. This is the very beginning of what will be your triumph. You are at a crossroads. Humanity is at a crossroads, as many of you know.

Right now, you *can* triumph and you *will* triumph through the work that you are all doing. All of you are progressing in one way or another. As you begin to work together in this, as you begin to work together in the evolution of the human species, you will progress much faster. Your progression will happen at an accelerated pace. As this progression happens at an accelerated pace, what you will find is that your triumph is your victory as humanity as one human species. This is why we are congratulating you now. This is just the beginning. You have much work to do. The human species has much work to do. This is the beginning of what will be a new Higher Human Being.

You now realize that your potential as a human being is much greater than you have ever known in the past. As you know this, as you know yourself working in tandem with God, you realize the capacity you hold for self-healing. Not just self-healing as an individual, but self-healing the collective human species and your physical landscape in your physical world. You do not need to worry about anything else.

As you heal the human species, your physical world will align. Your planet will align. The energetic grid of the planet that you will live in will align to the healing of the human species. This is how it will work. So, all you need is to work together. That is all you have to do from this point forward: work together.

Now, this is not easy for everybody. This is certainly not easy for people who are drawn and attracted to this type of work. However, this is not meant to be easy. You will find yourself a little uncomfortable in the process of having to work with others. But just know that this is a part of the process because you are breaking down forms and barriers, and that requires discomfort. But what you can know about this is that you have now reached a place where you are beginning to embark upon an entirely new frontier. This is the New Frontier, and this is where humanity is going.

You have now arrived at the understanding of the foundational concepts of *Project ONE*, and what will be brought to you next will be far more interactive. Now you may say, "This has been quite interactive; I've done a lot of work within this." Please understand that this will be far more interactive because it is going to take your participation to evolve. You cannot evolve through listening to a teaching, and you cannot evolve through meditating alone in a room any longer. This is not the way forward. The way forward is through conscious action, action within yourselves, actions toward each other and with each other. This is the practice being embodied in your life.

RECORD 40
YOUR HOMEWORK

Now, as we complete *Project ONE*, the foundational concepts; and as we complete this material, this work, what you have to know is that while you are asking yourself many questions about the work that you have come across, these questions will be answered in due time. You do not need to know everything today. All you need to understand today is the foundational concepts of *Project ONE* and to be able to sit and access the space. That is all you need to know today.

The questions that you are asking about the codes and the resonances, the various resonances that you will be working with and specifically the feminine resonance and all the other resonances that you will be introduced to ... you will come into understanding about these resonances as the material unfolds further.

Also, as far as the questions you have about codes and formulas that have been presented here ... you will also receive further information about this with the progression of humanity.

We are the ones bringing forth this information to you; therefore, we are monitoring your progression with the foundational concepts. You will receive information as you are prepared for it. This is a new topic for humanity, and this is new information coming forward. As such, it is important that you assimilate it into your being, one component at a time. This is what you have to know.

The formula will be laid out for you, and you will understand the feminine resonance and other resonances as you are ready to understand them. Right now, you simply need to understand these three foundational concepts that have been introduced to you in *Project ONE*.

This is important. As you assimilate this and as you are working with this material in groups and in partners, you will be given the rest of the information that you need to know. What we want to leave you with today and for you to understand before you progress forward is that the most important thing for you to do now is to understand these foundational concepts, to put this work into action; but also that this work, as we have said in the beginning, is going to require the use of your Free Will and God.

You must use your Free Will. Many of you have not chosen to use that yet. You will be asked to begin to claim that into being rather quickly in order to be able to do this work. Using your Free Will is the prerequisite for the rest of this project. Therefore, if you are having any trouble using your Free Will or understanding this concept, you will be able to talk among each other to be able to understand Free Will and to be able to claim your Free Will into being, because many of you *do* understand Free Will. Those of you who do are being asked to support others who do not. This is the first teaching that you will be able to work through together. You are being asked to work together on Free Will and to access your Free Will at all times.

We will progress further with codes in the next level, and the various resonances that you will be able to access.

Please know that you must choose love, and you must choose God. You must choose love and you must choose God in order to go forward with this work. It is the *prerequisite* for *Project ONE*.

This is the material you have been given so far, and this is what we will be ending with today.

ABOUT THE AUTHOR

Alison Storm experienced a spontaneous kundalini awakening in December of 2012 and has been integrating and working with that energy since that time. This energetic process allowed her to develop all of her intuitive senses to be able to support others on the path of awakening.

Today, Ali conducts events nationally, where she brings her energetic gifts as an intuitive/medium to others. She resides in New York City and Upstate New York with her family, where she maintains a private practice as a channel/intuitive and writer. She is unique in that she acts as a conduit to bring through wisdom and energy that is a catalyst for the awakening of others, and she helps others merge with their higher selves.

Website: www.alistorm33.com
Email: info@podelltalent.com

Made in the USA
Middletown, DE
15 July 2020